MORE
Letters to Uncle Mike

By
Michael Burgess

Saddle Mountain Press

ISBN: 0-9657638-6-2

First Edition

©Copyright 2000 Michael Burgess

Printed in the United States of America

Published by:
Saddle Mountain Press
P. O. Box 1096
Cannon Beach, OR 97110
Phone (503) 436-2947
Fax (503) 436-8635

Email: saddlemountain@upperleftedge.com

Cover designed by Anderson McConaughy, Portland, Oregon.

Acknowledgments

Fortunately for all concerned, writing is a solitary pursuit. Publishing is not. Several thankyous are in order.

First, to the Left Coast Group, a non-profit arts cabal operating, for all intents and purposes, out of Bill's Tavern in Cannon Beach, Oregon. I would like to say that, without their generous grant, this second volume of Letters to Uncle Mike would never have been written. That would be a bald faced lie. The letters come from a narrowly syndicated weekly advice column, *Ask Uncle Mike*, and were simply lying in a pile on top of my primitive computer. I have no idea how the Left Coast Group explained the grant to their accountant but, for the record, I applied by telling Billy Hults (the Group's executive director whose activities should probably be more closely monitored), that I was broke, I knew he had money and I wanted some. In return, I agreed not to relate several colorful stories of our 'business' trip to spring training in Phoenix and to call him sir whenever anyone important was around. Without the Left Coast Group's unflagging commitment to the arts, I would never have been able to do whatever it was I did with the money.

To Bob and Susann Ragsdale of Saddle Mountain Press who are, by professional standards, more fun than a barrel of monkeys. Susann's clear eyed pursuit of something else to laugh about is a perfect balance for Bob's whimsical approach to poker. They are very dear, if very odd, people for whom the literary world may well be ill-prepared.

Thanks also to Uncle Mike's many readers whose letters describing the startling mess they've made of their lives have lightened many a day and given him reason to go on. Pitiful, but there it is.

--Michael Burgess

This book is dedicated to my family and friends,
the greatest treasures of my life.

Introduction

Reader, this is the book. Book, this is the reader. Play nice.

MORE...

Dear Uncle Mike,
   You wrote something once about death and physics, how there couldn't be any really because the universe is always conscious. I think that's what you said. I was going to save it, but I didn't. Anyway, what about love and physics? A friend told me she heard that Einstein said that gravity wasn't love. If it isn't, what is? I'm 18 and would really like to know.
                                                    Emily in Portland

Dear Emily,
   Uncle Mike thinks Einstein was right and can only imagine how excited he'd be to hear it. Newton's gravitation was the mysterious attraction every piece of the universe has for every other. Relativistic gravitation is the curvature of space-time, the impersonal urge the universe has to curl up and be one with its navel. Neat as they both are, neither one is love. Uncle Mike sees love as phase entanglement. To review the basics. The universe is a four dimensional ripple tank. Observed reality is a standing wave pattern on a sea of unevoked possibility and we are wave packets: the sum and product of the invisible waves of our atoms stirred by invisible electrons dancing around our nuclei in the moonlight. Each human wave form is unique, a grand chord played on the ripple pond of awareness. The billions upon billions of waves making up the chord began when the universe first blinked and have been waving steadily ever since. Now comes the fun part. Each time a wave interacts with another, the experience changes

both of them, each leaving the encounter with a different energy and orientation. Or, in country western terms, a little piece of each other's hearts. They're both forever altered. The universe is a garden party of interpenetrating wave forms, humming and giggling and skipping along, merging, leaving bits of themselves with everyone they meet, taking bits to remember each other by. That's phase entanglement, a quantum intimacy exactly as old as time.

So much for mathematical elves and faeries. In the larger picture, you have us: human wave packets humming and whistling around a point conscious perspective, the much talked about 'I'. At our best we're extremely fine tuned and recognize right off the potential for harmony with other wave packets. That's love, Uncle Mike experiences it a lot when he drinks sour mash, and it exists to a greater or lesser degree, as an intrinsic relationship between all things. Some waves augment us, others interfere. The more the harmony, the more intricate the phase relationships and the deeper the resonance. Just like love, harmony depends upon difference. Harmony is the unification of difference balancing differences.

• • •

Dear Uncle Mike,

I've got a great wife but she does this one thing that drives me crazy. When we stay at a motel, she takes everything that's not nailed down. The soap, the shampoo, the shower caps, the matches, the note paper. It's like this ritual at check out time, she goes around the room picking up everything 'complementary'. Like I tell her, we can afford our own soap. She says everybody does it, we paid for it and it's ours. What do you think?

Bud R., Portland

Dear Bud,

Uncle Mike thinks your wife is a thief. And that her behavior violates the oldest of social rituals: the ceremony of the guest and the host. You come to the motel a stranger looking for shelter. You give your host a gift of money. In return, he or she provides everything necessary for your comfort. A warm, dry place to sleep,

2

cable television with remote, more than enough soap and shampoo, clean sheets, plenty of towels, and more than enough writing paper. This is why it's called the hospitality industry. Your responsibility as a guest is to treat your room not as if it were yours, but as if it were someone else's. You are obliged not to behave like animals, do disgusting things with the bed linen, or spray cheap champagne on the sofa sized painting. Such behavior is, or should be, beneath you. So it is with helping yourself to extra supplies. It doesn't matter whether the host has plenty more where that came from. If the little bars of soap were a gift, they'd be gaily wrapped and placed on your pillow.

• • •

Dear Uncle Mike,

My girlfriend is on me about the way I dress. I'm not a slob. I'm neat and clean but I just don't see any need to dress up. I figure any place where I can't wear Levis is someplace I wouldn't enjoy going. She knew I was like this before we got together. I've made my share of compromises and I think it's her turn. Come on man, back me up.

Your fellow guy, Beaverton

Dear Fellow Person,

Uncle Mike eagerly awaits the chance to back you up. And will, as soon as your thinking clears. For the moment, Uncle Mike regrets he can't be a fellow guy with you. As Uncle Mike understands your little non-issue, you refuse to dress up. Which, to you, means wearing any trousers that lack rivets. While charming behavior in a nine year old, this proletarian defiance lacks defense for adult guys, especially those involved in relationships with women (or, in your lexicon, adult gals). You must remember, Flippo, that even farmers and ranchers dress up. They don't do this because they want to. They do it because the women in their lives tell them to. There is nothing counter revolutionary in this. Women have been civilizing men since the invention of the cave. It may well be man's duty to resist being told when not to belch and scratch himself, but Uncle Mike would bet it was those who knew when to bring flowers whose genes have survived. So you

3

don't like to dress up. Very big deal. It's going to kill you to put on a sport coat and slacks and take the woman in your life to a restaurant where you order at the table? You say she knew your wardrobe, or lack thereof, before she blundered into the relationship. So what? She's supposed to live without hope that you'll grow up? Uncle Mike is a devout underdresser himself. The difference between you and he (and between you and most guys old enough to dress themselves) is that he enjoys pleasing the women who enjoy pleasing him. He also sees no reason to make his life a living hell over nothing.

· · ·

Dear Uncle Mike,

My class is making a list of the most influential people of the twentieth century. My teacher said it would be okay if I wrote and asked you. It's not cheating or anything. I'm eleven. Thank you.
Kristina L., Portland

Dear Kristina,

Uncle Mike is grateful for the opportunity to come up with his short list: Albert Einstein, Mahatma Ghandi, Muhamed Ali, and Bob Dylan. Einstein for his vision of relativity, Ghandi for his doctrine of passive resistance, Ali for showing us what it means to be a champion, and Dylan for pulling back the curtain and showing us the Great Oz in his underwear.

· · ·

Dear Uncle Mike,

I think I've got a problem. My boyfriend's ex-girlfriend is still part of his circle. This woman and I have never liked each other, wouldn't like each other whether we had a lover in common or not. There's nothing going on between them but they're obviously close and sometimes this makes me furious. I know it's stupid. I know it's jealousy over nothing. My boyfriend is getting fed up and I can see why. I know what I have to do, change my attitude and behavior. I guess what I'm asking you is, know any quick and easy ways to do this?
S.R., Reno

Dear S.R.,

Interesting words, quick and easy. Uncle Mike eagerly awaits any signs of quick and easy solutions to anything. There are quick and relatively easy actions which, if appropriate, lead to eventual solutions. Interesting word, solution. The first thing to do is separate your feelings from your behavior. There is no rule that says you must bond with this woman. There are rules that say you must, or at least should, be courteous and polite. You simply promise yourself you'll carry this off come hell or high water. Anything less than grace and charm is, or should be, beneath you. If, for no other reason, than that this woman is important to your partner. Will this be easy? Probably not. It can, however, be fun. Or at least entertaining. There's nothing phony about charming the socks off unpleasant dinner companions. It comes under the heading, or used to, of social skills. Even cow persons in sawdust saloons think twice about calling someone a polecat. Make the first move. Take her hand, or hug her with an acceptable level of insincerity, say it's nice to see her, then move on. She'll be baffled and you must resist the urge to take advantage. Behave impeccably while maintaining reserve. You're not trying to make a friend, you're eliminating an enemy. Changing your actions changes the system and her actions will change as a result. Next comes thought. Find something good about this woman (there must be something if your partner, a man of obvious good taste, was with her) and admit to yourself she's not the devil incarnate. When you think something negative about her, relentlessly balance it with something positive. It might help to say this aloud, in the bathroom, with your hand held over a candle flame. Change in thought will result in change of feelings. Mental activity is electromagnetic, quick and active. Emotions are biochemical states, slow to be flushed away and replaced by something more appropriate. With the right attitude, you'll begin to feel differently about her. Unless, of course, she turns out to be the cheap hussy you thought she was and confuses your lack of hostility with weakness.

• • •

Dear Uncle Mike,

I feel silly calling you uncle since I'm probably older than you are. I've been married for twenty-seven years and still my husband amazes me. We went to my sister's for a family reunion. Just about everyone was there. After dinner (we ate at about three), my husband asked my brother in law if he could borrow an upstairs bedroom for a nap. I was mortified. Right in the middle of things, he slips off for half an hour. I didn't know what to say to the family. And he still doesn't think he did anything wrong. You'll probably agree with him but I thought I'd give it a try. Dear Abby gets so many letters, she'd probably not answer.

Laura D., Seattle

Dear Laura,

Surprise, Uncle Mike thinks you're right about two things. Dear Abby probably wouldn't have answered your letter. She's very busy trying to help people with real problems. Uncle Mike is busy too, but he's a much nicer person. You're also right about who Uncle Mike sides with on the question of naps. Naps are a big part of the pursuit of happiness which means countless of his countrymen and women have died to defend his right to curl up with a blanket whenever he wants. Uncle Mike doesn't know your family. He can only hope for your husband's sake it's peopled with those who'd also agree you're full of beans. There's no item in the social code that says he can't slip off for a short snooze and Uncle Mike seriously doubts the festivities foundered as a result. If so, your family needs to be put to sleep. Feel free to try Abby for a second opinion.

• • •

Dear Uncle Mike,

My son is nine. He has a friend who's having a birthday party. The friend has a sister a year younger whose birthday is two days later. The party is for both of them and many of the children are planning to sleep over. I'm not sure about youngsters this age lolling around in their jammies watching videos together. I've met the parents only once. They seem nice, but who knows? Am I being old fashioned?

A Mom, Portland, Oregon

Dear Mom,

No dear, you're not being old fashioned. You're being ridiculous. You should be delighted your son and his friends even want to be in the same room with girl humans. Uncle Mike doubts seriously that the party will deteriorate into anything resembling the debauchery you imagine. If you want to play it especially safe, give your son a squirt gun and tell him to use it on anyone who suggests playing spin the bottle. Especially if they're in bunny pajamas.

• • •

Dear Uncle Mike,

I'm 24, my girlfriend is 22, we moved in together five months ago. She's really great and I love her a lot, we do all sorts of things together and we have a good sex life. I probably don't have a problem but here it is anyway. It's getting a little same-old same-old. We get up, we eat breakfast, we work, we eat dinner, we go out, we stay home, we go to bed. None of it's bad but it's routine, sometimes it's boring. I think she feels the same but she doesn't say anything. Actually, neither do I. I knew living together wouldn't be all skyrockets but I'm beginning to wonder if our chemistry is right. Maybe if we were with other people, it would be different. Maybe we're just in a slump. Who cares? I probably won't mail this anyway.

Don't Use My Name, Reno

Dear Don't,

Uncle Mike sympathizes with you. Not very much, but at least enough to take time from his jigsaw puzzle to slap some sense into you. He'll begin by congratulating you on your recent discovery of real life. Waking up, eating, working, playing, and going to sleep. That's it, cupcake. And it's much more than enough. Given moderation in all things, there's nothing wrong with routine. The daily ritual is a foundation that was old when our ancestors were discovering the use of the stick to open clams. The alternative to order is chaos, more exciting than routine, but most

7

times less fun.

You wonder if the chemistry between you and your friend is right. Interesting word, 'right'. If you haven't begun to hate each other by now, you can assume the chemistry isn't 'wrong'. It's just more familiar and, while familiarity needn't breed contempt, it often breeds complacence. 'Love' and 'life' aren't nouns, they're verbs, and anything not busy being born is busy dying. The truth couldn't be simpler. Every day is a day the universe has never experienced before. It and everything in it is creating itself as we speak. Uncle Mike wonders which part of this you find boring. Neither you nor your friend are the same people you were yesterday. And even if you were, it would still take you the next half of forever to get to the bottom of each other. In all his years of looking, Uncle Mike hasn't turned up anything more interesting than another human, unless it's poker. You wonder if your lives would be better if you were with other partners. Uncle Mike hasn't the foggiest notion. You can only count on it being different. As a musician friend once said of a band's breaking up so everyone could look for a better band, "The best band is the band you're in, two years from now." If you love each other, the best relationship is the one you're in, fifty years from now.

• • •

Dear Uncle Mike,

What's up with everyone and their dogs? It's like suddenly everybody has something large on a leash they're walking down the sidewalk while I'm trying to do my shopping or have a Danish and coffee. I like dogs, I just don't see why people have to walk them in places where the sidewalks are already crowded. I see old people all the time get nervous when a dog sniffs them, little kids get scared, the dogs get into fights, and whatnot. Shouldn't there be a law? Maybe I should just move to quieter neighborhood.

Alec, Portland

Dear Alec,

Uncle Mike is glad you got this off your chest. Should you move to a quieter neighborhood? We all should, pal. But we're where we are and that's that. People walk their dogs on Uncle Mike's sidewalks too. Uncle Mike separates them into two categories: those whose dog is their friend and boon companion and those whose dog is part of their new lifestyle. Unless their family has ancestral lands, Uncle Mike distrusts anyone with a matching brace of wolfhounds. Those barely restraining pit bulls within twenty yards of another living thing should be mauled and bitten by village elders. Should dogs be allowed on the footpath? Yes. It's their owners Uncle Mike would ban were he king. Contrary to the smug certainty on their faces, narrow concrete paths crowded with strange smelling humans and temptations for misadventure aren't the sort of venues dogs naturally seek out. They're like children brought to the beach so their parents can shop. Uncle Mike would also ban those parents.

• • •

Dear Uncle Mike,

My husband and I read your column and we're curious what you think about the recent cult suicides? I think it's not tragedy because they acted according to their beliefs. My husband thinks the leader was a whacko who persuaded a lot of innocent, not very bright people to kill themselves. Maybe you're sick of thinking about the subject, but we'd really be interested in your thoughts.

Joan and Roger S., Portland

Dear Joan and Roger,

Uncle Mike isn't at all sick of thinking about recent bizarre events in, of all places, southern California. Having given it so little thought thus far, he still feels fresh. Strictly speaking, and we really must, tragedy occurs when the great and noble are brought low by a character flaw. You're probably right to rule it out in this case. Uncle Mike has no quarrel with your husband's use of the term 'whacko'. Encouraging spiritual flowering to another plane is one thing, encouraging genital mutilation as a guarantee of sexual abstinence is another. Since Uncle Mike didn't know a one of them, he has no idea how innocent or bright they were. He'd personally have difficulty getting behind the notion that a flying saucer was coming for him and his friends in the tail of a comet. But then, he has difficulty believing Bill Gates is here to help us.

• • •

Dear Uncle Mike,

My boyfriend is into guilt trips. Nothing is ever quite right and nothing is ever forgotten. He doesn't expect me to be perfect, but it's close. This is my first live in relationship. If I'm patient and try, will he change? I love him a lot and don't want to throw it away, but I don't do well with guilt.

Annie L., Eugene, Oregon

Dear Annie,

Uncle Mike doesn't do guilt anymore. Uncle Mike does shame and embarrassment. He finds he can work with them. Guilt and innocence are simple statements referring to an act which either happened or not. The guilt you're talking about is truth wielded by those smarmy enough to remind you of it for the next half of forever. A story comes to mind. A monk and his student are walking in the forest. They come to a rain swollen stream. By the stream, a young woman ponders the crossing with uncertainty. The monk asks if he might carry her across. The young woman agrees. On the other side, their paths separate and the two men walk in silence for some time. The old monk finally asks the younger if he is troubled. The student nods. "In our order, we are forbidden to touch women. And yet you, my teacher, carried the woman across the stream." The old monk smiled. "Yes, but it is you who still carries her. I put her down long ago." It's a nice story but Uncle Mike would caution you against confusing yourself with a forest monk. Or your boyfriend with a rapt student. Simply put, he's a woefully insecure control freak who will, in all likelihood, make life a living hell for anyone lame enough to put up with it. If you're good, will the bad dream go away? No, the rules and standards will just change. This is a person who will never be satisfied because he believes very deeply that his glass can't be half full unless yours is half empty. You must refuse to accept this as normal behavior.

• • •

Dear Uncle Mike,

I read in the papers they're taking a look at cell phones and driving. I work in sales and couldn't do without one and find it hard to believe that using it makes me as great a risk as a drunk driver. Isn't this like a freedom of speech issue? Should the state be able to tell me I can't talk on the phone?

Jerry L., Coos Bay, Oregon

Dear Jerry,

No my little numbskull, this is not a freedom of speech issue. The state isn't telling you can't talk on a device that beams concentrated microwave radiation into your brain. That's up to you. The evidence just suggests that doing it while operating high velocity heavy equipment makes you a special kind of idiot.

• • •

Dear Uncle Mike,

I couldn't disagree more with what you recently wrote about guilt. If you do something that hurts someone you should feel guilty. Feeling ashamed is perhaps acceptable if the damage was small. Shame is for getting falling down drunk at the company picnic. Guilt is for sleeping with someone else's wife. If you can't do the time, don't do the crime. Wise up and quit handing out bad advice.

Cindy L., Astoria, Oregon

Dear Cindy,

Every day, something happens that makes Uncle Mike glad to be alive. Today, it's the fact he doesn't know you. Like funerals, guilt is for the benefit of the innocent, not the deceased. For every person wallowing in guilt, there's someone right there behind them pouring more slop in the wallow. Guilt depends on constant reinforcement, on not letting the fish off the hook. Aside from sadism, which Uncle Mike isn't into, there doesn't seem much point to the ritual. Especially since its logic flies, badly, against a simple physical truth: in all the universe, there's nothing more dead than the past. To feel guilty is to evoke remembered pain. Uncle Mike prefers to strike his forehead with a mallet. To encourage guilt in others is a hostile act. Depression is a physical state, a chemical imbalance in the brain that signals the body to, among other things, poison the immune system. It is quite possible to worry yourself to death.

Uncle Mike doubts that anyone has the right to muck about with his brain chemistry. He thinks they deserve a punch in the nose. The ends of things are in their beginnings and Uncle Mike has yet to see anything positive come from guilt. Shame is personal and redemptive, guilt is a debilitating social disease, not unlike the repeated casting of stones. My condolences to everyone who knows you.

• • •

Dear Uncle Mike,

I'm 18 and I really like your column. So do my girlfriends. I'm miserable. My boyfriend and I broke up a month ago. It was kind of both of our ideas. I felt confined and wanted to get out more, so did he. We're still friends. I really miss him and want him back. He's not really seeing anyone, I don't think. But he doesn't seem interested in getting back together. I haven't asked him or anything but he hasn't made any moves. My girlfriends tell me I'm being stupid to hold out for him. What do you think?

Marie C., Seattle, WA

Dear Marie,

Uncle Mike thinks you should listen to your friends. You could, of course, tell the young man your feelings. Uncle Mike's feeling is that this would be unpleasant for the both of you. At any given moment, we have what's ours. Wanting what isn't leads to pain and sadness. You have a friend. And a universe filled with interesting new ones. You'll find it's more than enough. Uncle Mike is glad you like the column. In his book, this makes you a person of unique, if questionable, taste. And your next young man a lucky lad indeed.

• • •

Dear Uncle Mike,

You seem to specialize in odd problems so here's one for you. My girlfriend and I are at an impasse. The issue? Pajamas. She doesn't want me to wear mine. She's always slept in the nude and thinks it's odd that I don't. I have no problem with nudity but I've always worn pajamas. She says I'll be more comfortable once I get used to it. I say I'm comfortable now and it shouldn't be an issue. Any thoughts? She says it won't matter whatever you say since you sound like a pajama person to her. She likes me anyway so don't take offense.

'P.J.', San Mateo, California

Dear P.J.,

For the record, Uncle Mike doesn't specialize in odd problems. Uncle Mike gets letters from odd people. So the little lady wants you out of your pajamas. Uncle Mike assumes the reason is not that your pajamas have bunnies or cowboys on them. You're absolutely right. This is an impasse. Next to naps, sleep is one of the most important activities of the day, and what we wear while doing it is a matter of immense personal importance. Uncle Mike also assumes you've given naked sleeping a chance. If not, you're a stick in the mud prig and you and your jammies deserve each other. If you've given it an honest chance and the experience turned out badly, you have an inalienable right to wear clothes to bed, and your bed mate has the inalienable responsibility to put a cork in it and go to sleep. So Uncle Mike sounds like a pajama person to her. Uncle Mike wonders what a pajama person sounds like. Even more, he wonders why anyone but the obsessive would care.

• • •

Dear Uncle Mike,

If a person drinks a lot, do they necessarily have a drinking problem? Am I an addict or just alcoholically over active?

Jenny in Portland

Dear Jenny,

You draw clever distinctions. Uncle Mike enjoys this in a human. Addiction, as Uncle Mike would bet you know, is a behavioral reflection of a chemical imbalance. Intoxication is a self induced chemical imbalance one is willing to pay money for. We purposely unbalance ourselves, or at least Uncle Mike does, because it makes us feel better. Wanting, or needing, to feel better is a human motive that comes right after the lust for experience and the will to survive. If you drink a lot, do you have a drinking problem? Maybe. Most people drink to put something to sleep. Sadly, it's often restraint and common sense. Played out too often socially, this can impact your life. Uncle Mike has no idea what sort of drunk you are. You could be witty and loads of fun. If so, you should remind yourself that, generally speaking, people are less interesting when they're speaking only in vowels. Like any drug, alcohol is a problem if it gets in the way of your life, if it keeps you from looking at yourself, if it separates you from people you love, if it interferes with the real work. Impromptu table dancing, getting sick in strange bathrooms, and waking next to someone you can't imagine having met are experiences that get in the way after a while.

· · ·

Dear Uncle Mike,

This girl I know and like a lot is having trouble with her boyfriend. We're both nineteen and have known each other for over a year. We get together for coffee and she tells me how unhappy she is, how he doesn't show her any respect, and yells at her. I've been listening to this for a month now and still haven't got up the nerve to tell her how I feel about her, that she should leave this jerk and be with me. My friends tell me she's just using me to cry on. What do you think?

B.L., Eugene, Oregon

Dear B.L.,

About what? This young woman is moaning and groaning to you about her relationship. Does this mean she wants out of it? No. It means she likes to moan and groan. If she wanted out of the relationship, you've probably made it more than obvious who she could call to help her move. Read nothing into the young lady's behavior beyond her willingness to share her half empty cup with you. As long as your stomach and patience hold up, your most appropriate action is to drink your coffee and listen. While you're listening, imagine yourself as the guy she's verbally vivisecting.

• • •

Dear Uncle Mike,

I saw something on the news the other night about 'dark matter'. I didn't quite get it. What is it and what does it mean? Is it like a black hole? Is it something I should worry about?

Brian S., Seattle

Dear Brian,

Uncle Mike always counsels against worrying. But then, you live closer to Bill Gates than he. As far as dark matter goes, you can put your mind at ease. No one quite gets it. Simply put, roughly 97% of the universe consists of something we can't see. Which is to say, a sort of massenergy we can't observe with the sort of massenergy we use to observe the reality we observe. We know the dark matter is there because, according to our figures, the galaxies are rotating more slowly than they should. What is it? Some species of mass that can't be observed with light. Some form of loosely coupled inertia. Something that's in the world but not, strictly speaking, of it. What does this mean? For one thing, that our knowledge of the universe is an incomplete understanding of 3% of reality. And that, just as quantum theory teaches, the observable creation is a thin froth of objectevents on the surface of a sea of unmanifest potential; the foam of 'what is' on the waves of 'what might be'. Uncle Mike finds little cause for worry in this. As for black holes, gravitational storm drains into which galaxies are sucked shrieking into a very real oblivion, we can't see them either. This is probably for the best.

15

• • •

Dear Uncle Mike,

My girlfriend and I have been going together for seven months. Last week, I asked her to marry me. She told me she needed time. Should I ask her again?

Darren L., Portland, Oregon

Dear Mope,

Only if you can't find a door to slam your fingers in.

• • •

Dear Uncle Mike,

I like your column a lot. You're Miss Manners with PMS. I want to have your children. Just kidding. Here's one for you. I want to go to a nude beach but my boyfriend thinks being naked around strangers is weird. I think he should at least give it a try. How pushy should I be? Have you ever been to a nude beach? Did you feel weird? Do you answer all your letters?

A Fan, Eugene, Oregon

Dear Fan,

Uncle Mike is beside himself to learn you like his column and is flattered at your comparison to Miss Manners. He tends to see himself as Ann Landers with gout. He's also relieved to hear you don't want to have his children. On to your episode of the human comedy. Should your boyfriend give nude beaching a try? One of Uncle Mike's first rules is that everyone gets to do what they want. Your friend has a cosmic, and constitutional, right to pursue happiness. If being buck naked around people he might avoid when fully clothed isn't his idea of fun, that's his affair. How pushy should you be? As pushy as you want, dear. Bearing in mind, of course, the relationship between action and reaction, and depending on how much you want to go to a tractor pull. Has Uncle Mike been to a nude beach? Yes, Uncle Mike has. Did he feel weird? Uncle Mike usually feels weird. Anticipatory unease is closer to the truth. Several hours of close observation, some of it shamelessly lascivious, left him with two new colors in his paint box. First, people are about as interesting with their clothes off as they are with their clothes on. Second, there are parts of your body that sun burn faster than others. Tell your boyfriend that, after several hundred beers, it will all seem quite normal. If your puppy still balks, tell him you're going without him. You ask, in closing, if Uncle Mike answers all of his letters. In his heart, yes. As a point of fact, Uncle Mike seldom answers his telephone.

· · ·

Dear Uncle Mike,

My little brother moved into town a few months ago so my wife and I agreed between us to offer him a place to stay while he got settled in. He's 29 and I'm 34, he's making a transition between banking and a stock brokerage. He's a good house guest, my wife likes him, and I love him like a brother. Now I remember he can be a little cheap. He got on with a brokerage two months ago making a thousand a month plus commissions. Not a lot of money. But that was two months ago and he's not mentioning moving out. I think it's about time but my wife gets all maternal and says we should let him build up his cash a little before throwing him to the wolves. If this were your brother, what would you do?

Ed in Portland, Oregon

Dear Ed,

Uncle Mike would put him up for adoption. You say his visit has reminded you that your brother can be a little cheap. You make no mention of his paying rent or buying groceries. If not, he's a usurious tightwad. Regardless, he's an insensitive lout who's stretched the social envelope about far enough. As his older brother, you must help him learn the lesson called 'no fair sponging'. Help the lad pack, tell him you're always good for a loan, and express eagerness to have dinner at his new apartment.

· · ·

17

Dear Uncle Mike,

The other night, my boyfriend and I went to what's supposed to be the best restaurant in town. It was sure as hell expensive enough. And very nice really. Midway through the meal, I looked over and this woman at the next table is eating her asparagus with her fingers. I almost choked on my wine. Nobody else seemed to notice except my boyfriend who couldn't believe it either. We're country bumpkins, right? This is legal, cuisine-wise?

Lisa O., Seattle, Washington

Dear Lisa,

Uncle Mike is wonderfully amused by your assumption he knows anything of the rules of fine dining, or as it's called on his block, haute eating. To Uncle Mike, the right fork is the one big enough to hold down his cheese burger. He does, however, have friends who collect and store bits of etiquette to use whenever they're feeling superior. Your question gave Uncle Mike a reason to speak to them. He was surprised and delighted to hear that asparagus is one of those foods which, like chicken legs, has been given the nod by the unseen masters of complicated eating. One must, of course, resist the urge to dangle and wave it while speaking.

• • •

Dear Uncle Mike,

Lately I've heard that obesity is a genetically determined imbalance. Does this make it a disease? It sure seems there are a lot of overweight people out there. A change in the gene pool?

Slim, San Francisco

Dear Slim,

Uncle Mike has no doubt that a metabolic tendency to heaviness can be an inherited trait. The term disease would, however, be no more appropriate than it is when applied to those who biochemically lean toward strong drink. We all have crosses to bear, the idea being to bear them. Your observation about an increase in corpulence among the citizens matches Uncle Mike's. Rather than a sudden evolution in the gene pool, Uncle Mike suspects a rise in overeating and boredom coupled with a surge in indolence and sloth. When you eat more than you need to and don't do diddley squat, you pork out. End of story. In closely related news, a person watching television burns fewer calories than a person doing absolutely nothing. Small surprise, researchers recently found a correlation between the amount of television a child watches and their belt size. Uncle Mike would bet his remote control the same holds true for adults. That overweight runs in families doesn't necessarily make it a genetic trait. It could be nothing more than dysfunction and child abuse. Since obesity is a leading cause of heart disease, a case could be made that over eaters are, aside from self indulgent, a drain on the health care system and an inflationary factor in insurance rates. Being a devout smoker, Uncle Mike would never suggest we hunt them down with pitchforks and deny them access to public areas.

• • •

Dear Uncle Mike,
    I'm thirteen, a girl, and I don't have a boyfriend. I've never really had one, just friends. Most of my girlfriends have one, even if they're not the kind of person I'd be interested in. There's this guy I like a lot, we just know each other. He's shy too but I think he likes me. My friends tell me I should let him know how I feel. I've tried and I can't. Should I wait for him to say something? I told my girlfriend I was going to write to you and she said you were probably too old to remember being young. She was just kidding.
                                Lonely in Eugene

Dear Lonely,
    Your snotty friend was right. Uncle Mike is too old to remember his youth and old enough not to care. This is what young people are for, to remind him that life could be more exciting and less amusing than it is. Fortunately, Uncle Mike doesn't need blissfully repressed memories to deal with your question. Courtship is a persistent ritual, older than dirt and common to insect societies. The gender two-step hasn't changed significantly

19

since we were marsupials; the music slows with the years but, for better or worse, the dancing never stops. Should you say something to your young man? This depends on two variables: what you plan to say and whether you're able to say it without choking on your tongue or dissolving into giggles. (A counter productive reflex that mellows with age but never goes away, and whose male version is no prettier. In time, you'll smile about it.) Uncle Mike doesn't recommend spilling your heart, and guts, to someone who is, at the moment, a nearly complete stranger. If he doesn't share your feelings, everyone will laugh behind your back, you'll die of embarrassment and your life will be ruined. Just kidding. It won't, however, be pretty. What you need now is more information. You need to know how he feels about you and you should surround him with opportunities to demonstrate it. Uncle Mike suggests this passive mode not because you're a girl human but because you're a girl human engaged in a courtship dance. The steps aren't gender specific. Give the lad subtle signals and wait for a less subtle response. Uncle Mike assumes you've been signaling already and that the object of your attentions is brighter than a brick and senses something's afoot. Being a boy human, he won't know what it is but there'll be time enough later for you to explain. Be attentive, interested, and mildly aloof. We're attracted most to what we don't understand and mystery is a large component of romance. Later, it's a large component of divorce. Welcome to the fun house. Uncle Mike wishes you much laughter.

• • •

Dear Uncle Mike,

I love my boyfriend but he does this one thing that makes me sick. He kills every insect he sees. He goes out of his way to stomp on ants, even outside, and will chase a fly around the living room for hours. Spiders don't last five minutes. This is not a violent man. He doesn't go hunting, doesn't eat much meat, and would never think of hurting an animal. But 'bugs' don't count. Is there something I can do to change him?

A bug hugger in Portland

Dear Bug Hugger,

There are many things you can do to change another person's behavior, most of them hilariously ineffective. Before Uncle Mike suggests one or two, he must congratulate you on finding a man who only does one thing that makes you sick. You're ahead of the game already. This said, what you're dealing with is a murderer. As a practitioner of unnecessary killing, your boyfriend is demonstrating a critical ignorance of reality. Sanctity of life is not a right reserved to humans. Contrary to what your little biopath seems to think, there aren't even chosen species. Life is life and even broccoli has rights. Aside from eating, and then only enough, we have no authorization from the Great Maker to kill anything. Yes, in a universe that's alive, it's not possible to 'kill' anything. But reducing an ant, a complex life form millions of years old when our ancestors were still lemurs, to a smear of organic chemicals by stomping on it is something that seldom occurs to those thinking clearly. What actions might you take to transform your friend into a responsible part of the creation? Buy a book on insects and shame him with tales of their social skills and elaborately functional lives. Give him a National Geographic video for his birthday. Explain that, if he'd allow spiders to roam more freely, the problem with flies and ants would largely solve itself. And that, if he persists in murdering innocent life forms, you'll give him a taste of rolled up newspaper. As you swat the back of his thick skull, murmur "Got him!" and smile sweetly.

• • •

Dear Uncle Mike,

Please say something about academia, something I can post on my wall to make me laugh. I am trying to read about Euripidean drama. Why are academics so dense? And please tell me a fun place to go to college, where the teachers are still human and it is like the sixties, except without all the stupid conflict (like the White Album done by Joan Didion), where people talk about things and are friendly, non-competitive, and enthusiastic. No, it's too late for me to go back to kindergarten. Please help.

Shirley in Kingman, Arizona

21

Dear Shirley,

You've presented Uncle Mike with a serious challenge. Of the much that can be said about academia, precious little of it is funny. Centuries ago, when Uncle Mike was at the university, the pomp and pedantry that seem naturally to drift, like swamp gas, over factories of higher learning were at least being seriously poked by the sort of questions that naturally come up during great social upheavals. Let the complacent say what they will about the sixties, it was a time when large ideas were in vogue. We live now in a time of small ideas; ideas so small they can be correctly confused with petty reactions. Historians will call this the time of the bean counters. Just as newspapers are now run by those who worked their way up through the sales department, the ship of academia is now largely run by those whose real talents are writing grants and training people to make money. Behind all the bells and whistles, universities have never been pretty. Their role in society is to preserve the dominant culture. Actively pushing the envelope of knowledge is something that happens mostly over coffee and pizza. The secret heart of academia lies in its architecture: what other part of life occurs in rooms where all the chairs except one are facing the same direction? Uncle Mike is glad you're reading Euripides, a very wise fellow; much wiser than the literature wonks who make their living explaining his tragedies two thousand years after the fact. Why are academics so dense? Because the audience they write for, future academics, admires and longs for it. Confronted with such dreck, Euripides would have got stinking drunk. As for the institutions themselves, Uncle Mike would love to think there are colleges where learning is still an enlightened activity, where the search for understanding has an energy and loft equal to the magic that was afoot in the justifiably notorious sixties. To be honest, he finds it much easier to believe that Bill Gates has our best interests at heart. The root meaning of the verb 'educe' is: 'to draw out'. This implies that the root of learning is inside the student. For Uncle Mike, education is the product of a good reading list, interesting people to talk to, and years of curiosity and unbridled wonder. It's reward is a life lived well, as opposed to one spent counting beans and watching HBO. Education is what you pay for. Learning is what you do. And none of us are too old for kindergarten. Play well.

• • •

Dear Uncle Mike,

Do you think motorcycle riders should be required to wear helmets?

Aaron L., Seattle

Dear Aaron,

In a word, no. It is, after all, their head. If they don't place value on it, that's between them and the universe. They should, however, be required to be organ donors and not count on priority service in the emergency room.

• • •

Dear Uncle Mike,

I had a dream with a dragon in it. Then I had a dream where I was a fairy, and then a dream with a tooth that was sort of like a shell, except it was a tooth and rather intricately designed. Is it a phallic symbol? What do these dreams mean?

Jelly Bean (not my real name), San Mateo, CA

P.S. The dragon gave me the tooth.

Dear Jelly Bean,

Of the many skills and talents Uncle Mike lacks, dream analysis is high on the list. This said, we wade in. Dragons are good because they need to be confronted. Dream dragons don't just hang out, whittling a stick or smelling flowers. They're windmills for the Sancho Panza in all of us. A chance to be flung down to the earth or up into the stars. Fairies (or, more correctly, faeries) are even better than dragons. Sadly, you failed to mention what kind of faerie you were. There's a different one for each element: fire, air, earth and water. There is, as you can imagine, a big difference between a gnome and a sylph. Teeth are for biting, for cutting through. Shells are the mothers of the pearl of creation (unless you consider the mollusk itself, which looks like the internal organs of a rock). And it's really an intricately designed tooth. So there you are, a faerie confronting a dragon who gives you an intricately carved tool for cutting through the shell of the Great Secret. Good job, kid. And you managed it without a single phallus.

• • •

Dear Uncle Mike,

My boyfriend invited some of the people he works with to our apartment for cocktails. I'm a little new to this. The invitations say 'from six to eight'. My boyfriend says we don't have to feed them because it's not a dinner invitation. It seems to me they'll expect something to eat. Should I at least have some cheese and crackers? There's a rule for this somewhere, right?

New in Town, Portland

Dear New,

There's a rule for everything somewhere, dear. But, since the massive framework of etiquette (a French word meaning 'ritual fussiness') was bolted together by people Uncle Mike would never allow in his home, he can be of no help telling you which rule applies to your situation. In Uncle Mike's experience, much of it too grisly to go into, food of some sort is a good idea at 'affairs de cocktail', especially when you ask your guests to show up at supper time. It makes no difference whether you're supposed to feed them or not. An evening of chitchat with people drinking on empty stomachs is an experience worth planning to prevent.

• • •

Dear Uncle Mike,

Does time really go faster when you're having fun?

Leah R., San Francisco

Dear Leah,

Strictly speaking, and we must, time doesn't go anywhere. Like space, time is a conceptual backdrop for perceived change. Or, more correctly, space-time is the fabric of creation, the warp and woof of observable reality. This doesn't, of course, mean that time is constant and unchanging. Space-time is related to velocity. As one's speed increases, one's wristwatch slows. At velocities approaching the speed of light, the time between clicks becomes, quite literally, half of forever. At the speed of light, space-time disappears, and with it, you and your clock. Does time go faster when you're having fun? This depends on what you mean by fun. Time goes fastest when you're sitting still. Unless you're watching television at the time.

. . .

Dear Uncle Mike,

I'm writing about a friend of mine. 'Joe' started seeing a woman about two months ago and his life's going down the toilet. She's a nice person and all, but she was dating another guy when she met Joe and she's still dating him. My friend's in love and having her go out with someone else is driving him nuts. All he can think about is how to win this woman. I'm afraid he's going to bump into the two of them some night and punch the guy's lights out. On nights when she's out with 'friends', Joe drives by her apartment to see if the lights are on and waits till she comes home to see who she's with. I'm worried about him. He doesn't listen to a word I say and says I don't understand what real love is. If you were me, what would you do?

A Friend in Seattle

Dear Friend,

If Uncle Mike were you, he'd pour himself a tumbler of sour mash and ponder the idiot mysteries of human behavior. Your friend says you don't understand real love. Uncle Mike's not sure he does either, but he does have a pretty good handle on mental imbalance and obsession, which is the sort of 'love' your friend is exhibiting to an outside observer. If and when he starts listening to you again, tell him for Uncle Mike that he's coming unwrapped over a situation that's none of his business. And, depending on the young woman's game plan, possibly beneath his contempt. After looking and looking for many years, Uncle Mike has yet to witness anyone winning someone's love. Falling in love is the least rational of all human pastimes and, unless the love object is a card carrying whacko, she or he won't be keeping score. We don't fall in love with winners, we fall in love with those it's impossible to resist. The young lady in question (your friend's emotional mess has youth written all over it) is doing what she wants. If she wanted to make a commitment to someone, she would. People are like that and your friend needs to recognize what is. And, as importantly, what isn't. Tell the nitwit that short circuiting will get him nowhere; unless the young lady is one of those who enjoy causing short circuits, in which case he and everyone else should avoid her like the plague. Encourage him to back off a bit, emotionally disengage, lower the voltage. Offer to help by strapping him to a kitchen chair and giving him a towel to chew on. Explain that he's being a hopeless mope and needs to stiffen his spine. Tell him that with love, as with the rest of life, the only way to win is by deciding not to compete. And that driving by someone's apartment and parking there in the dead of night to see who she comes home with isn't just obsessive. It's a form of stalking.

• • •

Dear Uncle Mike,

I'm a woman in my mid twenties. My boyfriend and I just moved in together. When we each had our own place, I was impressed that Rocky (not his real name of course) not only kept his own apartment clean, he also shared cooking and dishwashing when he stayed over with me. My friends told me how lucky I was. Now, I agree. Since we moved in together, he's become a different person. Somehow, it usually works out that I cook (he says my cooking is better than his and I can't argue) and do the bulk of the clean up. He's not a slob and picks up after himself but that's about it. When it comes to real house work (deep cleaning, the toilet), he dawdles and putters until I tell him to just get out of the way. We've talked about it, he knows I'm not happy with the arrangement and he keeps saying he'll try harder. So far, talk's been cheap. He says since I only work 30 hours a week and he works at least 40, it's only fair that I put more time into the house work. I bring in as much money as he does and I figure the extra time is mine to do what I want with. Who's not being fair here?

Being Had, Sausalito

Dear Ms. Had,

It's a close call, but you win. Which is to say, you're slightly more off base than your less than gallant lout. To be played well, the domestic comedy must be reduced to simplest terms. Beginning with our descent from trees, human society has been arranged around two kinds of work: that which is done inside the cave and that which is done outside. We may have prettier foreheads than our ancestors but we remain hunter gatherers, dragging home paychecks instead of antelope. For biological reasons too politically incorrect to mention, the lady hunter gatherers mostly stayed at home while the men of the house went out and killed something. This done, their work week was over. (Anthropologists recently decided that, in order to sustain the family unit, the average hunter gatherer labored about four hours a week, spending the rest of their time playing the flute, horsing around with the kids, and chatting. The industrial revolution rescued us from this.) So much for tradition. Recent changes in society—the take over of the planet by ruthless corporations, the institutionalization of greed, and the invention of the two wage earner family—has bulldozed the playing field. Gender equality has empowered us all to become professionals, defining ourselves by how well we do hunting and gathering dollars in the marketplace. Nobody's home, not even the kids. It's a pretty funny world. But we were talking about you. You make the same money as your partner in less time. Good for you. Regardless of your sex, this means you have more time for inside work. No, you shouldn't spend all of your extra ten hours scrubbing out the bathtub, just as (nudge, nudge) you wouldn't expect your sweet baboo to. Neither should your shameless male imagine that whining is a substitute for sharing unpleasant chores. Remind him he's a big, strong man and can take it. Another possibility is for the two of you to drag back enough antelope to afford a house cleaning service.

• • •

Dear Uncle Mike,

Just one simple question. How old are you? My friend thinks you're over fifty, I think you're younger. We're both eighteen. Also, what do you look like? Why don't you have a picture with your column? I'll bet a lot of people are curious who you are.

Amy and Maria, Eugene, Oregon

Dear Amy and Maria,

Many people are curious who Uncle Mike really is, none of them more than Uncle Mike himself. As for age, you're both right. Depending on the day, Uncle Mike is either younger than springtime or older than dirt. What does Uncle Mike look like? Your basic male human, except for the feathers. The feathers explain why no photograph runs with the column.

. . .

Dear Uncle Mike,

Could you give your readers a sure fire, polite way to say no to invitations? I couldn't come up with a good one on the spur of the moment last week and spent one of the most miserable nights of my life eating bad home made Szechwan in the company of people I wish I hadn't met. Stop me before I say yes again.

Can't Say No, Seattle

Dear Can't,

Since the only thing worse than being invited too often is being invited rarely or not at all, the art of declining gracefully is a crucial stitch in the social fabric. Over the years, Uncle Mike has experimented with many excuses, his early failures including: "Darn, my aunt is dying that night", "I'd sooner be staked out in a crab pit", and "I've taken a vow of nudity." The important part of declining is that your reason, whatever it is, must contain at least a shred of truth. Uncle Mike's generic fade back position is that he'd love to, and would, if he weren't going out of town. Sometime on the appointed day, Uncle Mike goes to the city limits, stops at the first diner and has a cup of coffee and reads the New Yorker. It also works with cheap novels.

Dear Uncle Mike,

My older sister's kid is driving the family nuts. She's seven and has to be the center of attention. If I stop by for a visit, Tiffany (yes, that's her real name) plants herself between my sister and I and takes over the conversation. If that doesn't work, she stands in front of us, tap dances and expects applause. If her mother tries to ignore her (a real rarity), she tugs on her clothes and all but crawls into her lap. Forget about sharing a meal. The little subhuman treats her parents like hired help and the guests like people who've come to watch and praise her. Yes, she's smart and has a sweet side, but it's getting to where I don't even want to visit. The rest of the family feels the same. My sis says Tiffany's talented and precocious. We think she's spoiled rotten and her folks are headed for real trouble. I don't have children and so my opinion's not worth a lot, especially to an older sister, but we were raised to have manners and this kid's a tyrant in tap shoes. Any suggestions?

Fed Up in Portland

Dear Fed Up,

Assuming the family has ruled out signing your sister up for electroshock, Uncle Mike suggests you concentrate your energies on little Tiffany. It takes a whole village to raise an obnoxious child and, as her elders, you owe the little whelp your wisdom about the ways of the world. One of those ways is the relationship between adult and apprentice humans. (Referring to her as 'subhuman' seems harsh, but then Uncle Mike has the good fortune of not knowing her.) Pick a quiet moment when you and little Tiffany are alone. Look her dead in the eye and explain that if children were meant to rule the planet, the universe would have made them larger and more clever than they are. Tell her that, although you love the time you spend together, you wish she'd spend less time entertaining and more time playing quietly by herself. That, unlike her mother, but like everyone else in the world, your love for her isn't even close to unconditional. And that, if she's a good little girl and really tries to let others get a word in edgewise, you won't shove a sock in her mouth and duct tape her dancing feet together.

Dear Uncle Mike,

What are your thoughts on the McVeigh thing? Do you think the guy's being railroaded? Guilty or innocent?

E.P., Coos Bay, Oregon

Dear E.P.

As in the case of O.J. Simpson, Uncle Mike doesn't know the young man, wasn't in Oklahoma City on the day in question, and avoided, with nearly complete success, the breathless reportage of the trial like the plague of press releases it continues to be. Never have so many imagined they knew so much about affairs that weren't their own. As for guilt and innocence, you've got the wrong legal system. In court, one is either guilty or not guilty; innocence is neither a consideration nor an acceptable plea. Whatever happened, Uncle Mike longs for anything that will bring 'closure': a process indistinguishable from the old fashioned 'getting on with your life' except that it takes much longer and is more vocal. The only bright side to the affair is that, since Mr. McVeigh was not good at running while carrying a ball and has starred in no television commercials, the number of civil suits will be smaller. After you strip his parents of their retirement, what have you got?

• • •

Dear Uncle Mike,

I will make this letter as pleasant as possible. As a practicing counselor, I'm curious: do you honestly feel you're up to the responsibility of dispensing advice to people you've never met? Do you have any formal training in psychology? I read your column infrequently. Even so, there have been several occasions when I felt your advice was more clever than therapeutic. If you were seeing me professionally, I'd explore with you the possibility that you're overcompensating for an inability to manage your own affairs and are merely seeking attention and ego fulfillment. Care to respond? Or, better yet, schedule an appointment?

A Mental Health Professional, Spokane

Dear Mental,

Because Uncle Mike senses in you a pressing need for order, he'll answer your questions in the sequence they were presented. Does Uncle Mike feel up to giving advice to strangers? You bet. Ann Landers and Dear Abby get away with it and they're writing from another century. Does Uncle Mike have any formal training in psychology? Absolutely not. He studied literature, a field in which abnormality is encouraged rather than medicated. Uncle Mike also studied psychology majors and found them alarmingly odd. Uncle Mike is happy to hear you read his column infrequently and would recommend, professionally, that you cut back even further. As a replacement, explore the Sunday funnies and, in severe cases, cartoons in the New Yorker. Uncle Mike is delighted that you found some of his advice more clever than therapeutic. Increasing your dosage will make much of this go away. Your theory about overcompensation, personal inadequacy, and a starved ego yearning to be listened to is, in Uncle Mike's professional opinion, a real dandy and he plans to give it all the thought it deserves. He regrets not being able to schedule an appointment with you. He's afraid it might be more therapeutic than clever. Have a normal day.

• • •

Dear Uncle Mike,

You've got an opinion about everything so what do you think about the comet Hale-Bopp? My boyfriend says it's like a sign of the coming millennium. I say it's a big snowball and doesn't mean anything. Remember Kahoutek? Did I miss the wondrous happenings?

Linda in Walla Walla

31

Dear Linda,

You've dealt Uncle Mike an unfair blow. Uncle Mike does not have an opinion about everything. He's absolutely mum on Sanskrit poetry and keeps pretty quiet about cooking. You have, however, struck a vein with comets. We need to keep in mind that comets come in two types: those that return on closed elliptical orbits, and those that don't. The ones that don't are one time postcards from the universe, beautiful if only for the random nature of the encounter, celestial bodies passing in the night. Comets on elliptical orbits are another matter. Their predictability makes them part of the clockwork, a regularly recurring ripple in the wave pattern of the solar system. Do they mean anything? Uncle Mike would ask what doesn't? Do they affect history? History, bless its heart, seems to repeat itself, as if it occurred in cycles rather than straight lines. Uncle Mike finds no reason to disbelieve that the cycles of comets and the cycles of human and geological events could be in some sort of synch. Halley's comet has a rather lurid historical past and, as for Kahoutek, the great disappointment of 1973, something more than a score of world governments underwent radical change in the year following its fizzle. But all this is beside the point. It's the nature of comets that is their meaning. We've recently learned that small cosmic snowballs by the scrillions vaporize in our atmosphere every day. According to the numbers, they could, over scrillions of years, have accounted for all the water on the planet. Then the big boys sail by with their magnificent tails and spew organic molecules onto the waves. Uncle Mike thinks this is pretty sexy stuff. He has an opinion about that too.

• • •

Dear Uncle Mike,

I'm thirteen. Is it okay to ask a boy to a party? Some of my girlfriends think it's not. Some of them think it is. Does this scare boys off? What do I do if he says no? Can you remember when you were young?

Kris in Eugene

Dear Kris,

While Uncle Mike can remember much of his youth, he chooses not to. Being not young is far too involving and much more fun. Is it okay to ask a boy to a party? You should do whatever it is your nature to do. That you're a girl human should have nothing to do with making friendly gestures toward boy humans. Does this scare boy humans off? Some of them. But then, some of them are too easily startled for their own good and it's your duty as a girl human to gently unbalance them. What do you do if he says no? You hurt, dear, and go off and nurse your wounds. Your fear of rejection is not gender specific. It is, in fact, a main ingredient in the skittish behavior of males of all ages. If you choose to fall back on biochemical tradition, Uncle Mike suggests you surround the lad with your interest, behaving in subtle ways that will eventually make persuading you to go to a party with him his sole mission in life. Have fun and play nice.

• • •

Dear Uncle Mike,

Okay, one more time. In simplest possible terms, could you tell me why you don't believe in death. You've talked about it before in terms of quantum physics and I almost follow you. It stops about an inch in front of my forehead. Once more, in one syllable words?

Richard in Portland

Dear Richard,

Okay, ready set? Whether you call it quantum probability or the holy ghost, the universe exists as something more than what we can see and measure. At this level, the universe itself is a life form; trees and galaxies and Paris in the spring are all gross reflections of the potential, or spirit, of the creation. The playing out of pattern, the word made flesh, the nominative of the verb 'to be'. Uncle Mike's place in this, his biological clock aside, is that of a point conscious observer: a perspective of the universe unique and undying, a riff in the jazz of spacetime, the present position of a time line that, like every other perspective, started with the big bang. For the universe to be complete, each perspective must endure. Unfortunately for all concerned, some of these perspectives make unpleasant dinner companions at a feast that goes on forever. Sorry about the polysyllables, Dick.

• • •

Dear Uncle Mike,

My sister is 31 and has a nine year old son. She's divorced and has been single parenting for five years. Her husband was a real snake, the relationship between them was horrible then, it's not good now. His relationship with his son is one of irregular visits. The kid doesn't like the visits much and is leery of his father, justifiably since the (vivid expletive deleted) is harsh, judgmental, and sarcastic. Here's why I'm writing. The separation and divorce was messy and the boy slept a lot with his mom. He was four then and it was understandable. He still sleeps with her. I understood it was only every once in a while and that was odd enough. Now I find out it's like two or three days a week. I love my sister a lot and the kid's a good kid, shy and insecure but smart and polite. I know that different people have different emotional needs and that I'm no one to pronounce on others' lives, but this seems a little weird to me.

A Brother in Beaverton, OR

Dear Brother,

Having observed, and played badly in, many performances of the human comedy, not much strikes Uncle Mike as weird anymore. Your sister, bless her heart, manages to make the cut. Unless they're marooned in a snow cave, or there's a legitimate concern that one or both will die in their sleep, no nine year old boy should sleep with his mother. Uncle Mike wouldn't touch your sister's emotional agenda with a ten foot pole, the kindest thing to be said is that she's horribly misguided and tragically self absorbed. An important prerequisite to life as an adult human is self-integration: a process that begins with the umbilical cord, progresses through bathroom etiquette, and leads, sooner rather than later, to independent sleeping arrangements. Uncle Mike never invokes the concept of normality but, for the average 31 year old woman and the average nine year old boy, sleeping in the same bed is a thought that seldom, if ever, occurs. If we're looking for a psychobabble catch phrase, 'arrested development' will do nicely. In your sister's case, it's one arrested development arresting another's; selfishness, loneliness and need masquerading as love. It's a funny world. It would be less funny if the people we're talking about were a 31 year old man and his nine year old daughter. Uncle Mike would be interested, mildly and from a distance, to hear your sister's take on that domestic tableau. Uncle Mike also wonders how you see your role as the lad's uncle. Your sister's needs aside, your place as a male elder is to help guide apprentice young men along the booby trapped path to adulthood. This includes taking him camping, teaching him how to make fire, and telling him he's too old to be sleeping with his mother.

· · ·

Dear Uncle Mike,

My girlfriend's giving me a hard time about this party we didn't go to. She says I should have called to cancel. It was a good sized party and I figure if we didn't show, we didn't show. If my girlfriend's right, don't answer.

Erin in Eugene, OR

Dear Erin,

Before beginning, let Uncle Mike say you sound like a real piece of work. Although simple, your question poses a challenge. The quick answer, for those not raised in a family of dysfunctional weasels, is yes, you should have called to decline the invitation. You should even, you might want to sit down, have offered a plausible reason for not attending and said thank you for being invited. But, in your own special way, you're right. That you even asked the question implies that anyone who'd invite you to their home wouldn't expect such graces, and that the party probably wasn't maimed by your absence. Give your girlfriend my sympathies.

Dear Uncle Mike,

I'm a woman, 28, and I'd be interested in your thoughts on women who don't shave their legs or underarms. I say you'd be more the smooth type, my best friend thinks you're a natural, liberal kind of guy and it wouldn't matter. I should tell you she has a lot more faith in you than I do.

"Thelma & Louise", Portland

Dear Ladies,

Uncle Mike is uncertain what sort of faith would be founded on female body hair or its lack, but is nonetheless pleased to hear one of you has it. Faith of any sort is in short supply these days and even the flimsiest add up. You ask Uncle Mike's thoughts, here they are. If women want to shave their legs and armpits, they should do so. If they don't, they shouldn't. Although Uncle Mike is not a liberal kind of guy, he would defend either position; not to the death, mind you, or even to harsh words, but defend them nonetheless. You invoke the word 'natural', which Uncle Mike takes to mean anything of or pertaining to nature. Shaving one's armpit is as natural an occurrence as not shaving it. Uncle Mike shaves much of his face every day and still feels remarkably natural. Does Uncle Mike have a personal preference? Would everyone who doesn't raise their hand? Nearly without exception, the women who've pirouetted through Uncle Mike's life chose to practice self depilation. It's possible he unconsciously sought them out. A victim of his childhood, Uncle Mike's first love goddesses were Donna Reed and Annette Funicello.

• • •

Dear Uncle Mike,

I keep hearing how girls are as sexual as guys. Somebody should tell my girlfriend. None of the girls I've dated, I'm 19, are that much into it. Don't tell me it's me because some of my friends say the same thing and the girls say it's not me, it's them. I think it's a bunch of feminist propaganda that sells lipstick and sexy lingerie. Girls don't like sex as much as guys. They use it. That's a fact.

A Guy in Phoenix

Dear Guy,

Thanks for writing. Uncle Mike sometimes forgets that men like you still exist outside of made for television movies. Because of you, he'll be able to nod and smile again at bumperstickers that say 'Boyfriend In Trunk'. On now to your hilarious premise that girl humans don't like sex as much as guy humans. Girl humans, when sexually provoked, eat boy humans for lunch. Being who you are, you may well never experience this. What most women aren't into, Cupcake, is sex without love. As someone, probably a woman, observed: the largest sexual organ is the brain. Using this standard and judging from your letter, you're a walking bundle of dysfunction. Please take this personally. For women, and those men with emotional IQs in the double digits, sexual pleasure is more dependent upon context than content. Making love is a continual, shared process that periodically results in orgasm. As opposed to having usurious sex, which is what you do with young women too inexperienced to know the extent of your lameness or too polite to laugh. The results of a recent study of teensomethings conducted by Ohio State University's Center for Human Resource Research found that adolescent males who aren't sexually active are more likely to be depressed than the even more adolescent males who are, as you and your smarmy buddies would say, scoring like bandits. On the other hand, adolescent females who are sexually active are more likely to be depressed and feel like failures than those with no sexual experience. The researchers concluded that young girls who don't feel good about themselves look for security and self esteem through sexual relations. And what do they find? Selfish, shallow, clueless dildos like you who couldn't make love if the directions were written on their skateboard. You are, bless your little punkin head, right about one thing. Women do use sex. The nice ones use it to teach men how to love.

• • •

Dear Uncle Mike,

My girlfriend says it's bad form to blow on your soup. I say it beats burning your lips. Is there a rule about this? Who made it?

Slob and Snob, Portland

Dear Slob and Snob,

Like many others, you've confused Uncle Mike with Miss Manners. Uncle Mike knows nothing of table etiquette aside from his nearly always correct use of the napkin. Should one blow on one's soup? If done gently and decorously, Uncle Mike can't see why not. But then, Uncle Mike sees nothing wrong with wiping up gravy with one's biscuit. You should not, of course, blow on the soup of others, even when asked. Unless they're rolling your sock down with their toe. The rules of soup blowing were most likely hammered out by the French whose word 'etiquette' means 'manners for the pretentious'.

• • •

Dear Uncle Mike,

I read your column all the time. I like you, you're weird. A while back, you described yourself as a 'born again Pythagorean'. What exactly does this mean? Do you have a fan club? Can I join?

Diandre S., Seattle

Dear Diandre,

Among other things, Pythagoras taught that the root of all things is number, that the world we observe is a shadow play of proportions, chords, and harmonies. Pythagoras, who spent a long time thinking about it, felt that numbers were as much qualities as quantities. The geometry of the triangle is what happens when the quality of 'threeness' encloses space. The geometry of the circle, a figure of infinite sides, revealed to Pythagoras something that's in the world but not of it. Draw a circle. Any circle. Now, divide it in half with a line. If you say the length of this diameter is one, or unity, then the length of the circumference is an irrational number: an endless decimal term. The physical universe thus becomes an order imposed upon irrationality, uncertainty, and chaos. Since this aligns nicely with the precepts of both Buddhism and Quantum Mechanics, Uncle Mike would feel a fool not to embrace it. He also respects Pythagoras' approach to education.

For the first five years, pupils at his academy weren't allowed to speak. The theory being that until they'd watched, listened, and thought that long, they really had nothing to say. Does Uncle Mike have a fan club? No. Can you join? Absolutely. In a quantum universe guided by an irrational series, whatever can happen but hasn't eventually will. It will happen faster if you send Uncle Mike a fat check.

. . .

Dear Uncle Mike,

I read your excellent column in the Elko Daily Free Press and you crack me up. First let me say I am an uncle and also a Mike so I know where you are coming from. In fact I am so knowledgeable (aren't all Mike's?) that I know all of the answers to all the cosmic riddles (except one) so if you ever get stuck on a question I will be glad to help.

Truly, Michael T., Crescent Valley, Nevada

P.S. The only mystery to me is why rest room doors push in when you do not care about your hands but pull open after your Biz is done—most people as you may know do not wash, I do—solution? Wash and dry then use the paper towel to pull on the handle, discard, next question?

Dear Michael,

Uncle Mike is glad he cracks you up. He gets a kick out of you too. He's glad too that you're an uncle, and a Mike, and so know where he's coming from; a place which, like every other point conscious perspective in the universe, is intimately related to wherever it is he's been. He's especially glad you know the answers to all the cosmic riddles except one. There can't be many of you around and Uncle Mike figures you're going to come in real handy one day. Pressing on to your last remaining mystery: why do rest room doors open in? First off, Uncle Mike questions that they all do. He can remember at least one night, fueled by hundreds of gin and tonics, when an outward opening men's room door struck his forehead like the hand of an angry god. That he was on his hands and knees at the time only makes the memory more indelible. But if you say rest room doors swing in, Uncle

Mike is happy to jolly you along. Since hinges can be attached to either side of a door, preference probably reflects either building codes or some ancient carpenters' tradition. Uncle Mike doubts the latter since, when he was a lad, the outhouse door swung out. This is an ancient tradition based on the discovery that there wasn't enough room for it to swing in. Trial and error is a harsh teacher. With public out houses of more lavish dimensions, it seems only fair that, if anyone gets a face full of door, it should be those who have found relief rather than those still desperately seeking it. But your concerns were for hygiene and public health rather than safety and humanitarian architecture. Try as he might, Uncle Mike cannot join you in your fear of door handles. First, because he long since realized that, shower as often as we want, we're still just walking petri dishes for microbes you'd have a hard time killing with a blow torch. Second, because he already has enough on his plate coming to grips with irrational numbers. Uncle Mike will say that the solution you've come up with for your septic problems, while not likely to win a Nobel, sounds like a dandy. He does have one question: how, while standing at the disease infested door, does one dispose of the protective (we really should talk) paper towel? Does one fling it toward the trash can or hand it to the person coming in? What if the person is wearing surgical gloves or is wrapped in sterile gauze?

• • •

Dear Uncle Mike,

What is it exactly that you have against the French? I'm of French ancestry and I take offense at your snide comments about French cuisine and etiquette, which you called "a French word meaning manners for the pretentious". Surely you don't think that cooking with attention to detail is bad or imagine that the French invented the rules of etiquette by themselves. You would not, I'm sure, enjoy someone deriding your ancestry and I think you should give second thought to deriding the ancestry of others.

Michelle S., Portland, Oregon

Dear Snotty French Person,
Uncle Mike has nothing against the French. Au contraire. Uncle Mike feels that, if the French didn't exist, history would have been forced to invent them.

. . .

Dear Uncle Mike,
Last week my husband brought home an adult video. We'd talked about it and I agreed, partly from curiosity and partly to please him. It was about what I expected only more so. I wasn't disgusted and was even aroused by some of the scenes. I hadn't expected that. Our lovemaking was, to put it lightly, spirited. That was certainly okay with me. Now, I'm trying to process the experience. I don't know how I feel about expanding my sex life to include professional actors and actresses. And I confess feeling a little weird about sharing an experience with the guys in overcoats in the adult video stores. I'd be interested in your thoughts.
Curious Yellow in Astoria, Oregon

Dear Curious,
What you're dealing with here is a taboo. Every society has them, and a large portion of ours have to do with sexuality. Go figure. While few things are uglier than full-blown hedonism, Uncle Mike has much respect and fondness for the pleasure principle. Your sexuality is your business. Your body is a reflection of your spirit and no rules governing its use can be made by anyone but yourself. If you were aroused by images of sexual coupling, you were aroused by images of sexual coupling. Uncle Mike assumes you enjoy being aroused and believes that whatever improves lovemaking between wildly consenting adults violates no rule of the universe he's aware of. As for sharing an experience with other perverts who dress differently and frequent shops you don't, Uncle Mike would caution against it.

. . .

41

Dear Uncle Mike,

I've got a problem with my neighbor. She's a young woman in her early twenties and lives in the building across from mine. She's very attractive, exercises a lot, spends a lot of time without many clothes on and never pulls the drapes. I'm not a peeping Tom but since her apartment is on the same level as mine, she's pretty hard to ignore. I work at home and, without really meaning to, I've become familiar with her schedule and have started arranging to be home at certain times. It's not an obsession or anything but I'd be lying if I said I don't look forward to watching her walk around in the nude. My girlfriend's pretty cool about it and kids me about being a pervert but if she knew how much time I spend at the window, she'd definitely be (upset). At first I didn't feel guilty. I mean, if she's comfortable with the blinds up, why should I feel bad about watching her? Now I don't know. I'm starting to think about her a lot. A buddy of mine has warned me not to get caught, that watching people when they don't know you're watching them is against the law. Is this true? If you were me, what would you do?

Bloodshot in Seattle

Dear Bloodshot,

If Uncle Mike were you, his eyes, and his moral code, would be every bit as strained as yours. But Uncle Mike isn't you and has no regrets about it. First off, you're probably breaking no laws. To be a full fledged peeping Tom, you must go out of your way. Arranging to be home at certain times doesn't count. You're merely an ogler and a sneak whose girlfriend should go upside his head with a skillet. Instead of looking at your neighbor as a gift from a kind universe, look at her as someone who's dangerously oblivious to a reality that includes you, your binoculars, and your torrid little fantasies. Just because the woman has little sense of privacy doesn't mean it's okay for you to methodically violate it. Life's filled with temptation, chum, and resisting it is its own reward. Whenever you feel the call of the voyeur, hold your hand over a candle flame until you remember there are nobler things you could be doing. Buy yourself a handsome set of blinds and, whenever possible, be somewhere else during the floor show. Uncle

Mike would suggest a nudie bar where, for better or worse, everyone knows the script. You could take your girl friend along just to test the level of her coolness. If all else fails, you could move and sublet your place to Uncle Mike.

. . .

Dear Uncle Mike,

Do you have a good method for discouraging unwanted visitors? We live at the coast and have a hard time coming up with new reasons for not serving as a motel for friends and family. We don't want to be rude but when you live in a vacation spot, people tend to take advantage.

G.S., Florence, Oregon

Dear G.S.,

Uncle Mike wishes you luck. For those whose conscience allows minivacationing in the homes of others, few methods, short of firing a round or two over their heads, will dissuade them. Uncle Mike is much charmed by your desire not to be rude and wishes you even more luck. As for personal methods of discouragement, Uncle Mike isn't a real gold mine. Owing to his love for barnyard imitations, he has few repeat visitors. You might tell the shameless louts about the massive bloom of poisonous plankton, or the unexplained rash of sea gull attacks, or the fire that recently gutted your home. Or suggest they rent an ocean front suite so you can get away too.

. . .

Dear Uncle Mike,

My girlfriend is thinking about getting one of those little pot-bellied pigs. I have my doubts. The brochures say they're clean and smart. Do you know anything about pigs? Do they get along with cats?

Chris T., Eugene, Oregon

Dear Chris,

Although Uncle Mike loves all creatures great and small, he shares your doubts about living with a pig. Granted, pigs are intelligent. So are many of Uncle Mike's acquaintances and he's in no way tempted to live with them. As for personal hygiene, a pig who bathes regularly will be no more unsightly or unpleasant than a bald dog who snorts a lot. It will, however, be a pig with unfulfilled dreams. Like their near kin, the hippopotamus (a notoriously bad pet), pigs have a genetic urge to wallow. If your conscience won't permit thwarting your pig in its quest to be all it can be, you'll need to convert a portion of your back yard into a mud pit. For those living in apartments, a plastic wading pool filled with topsoil can be tucked into the spare bedroom. This, and a hose, will be all your new roommate needs.

. . .

Dear Uncle Mike,

My problem is with you. My wife thinks you're God on wheels. She reads your column to me at the damn breakfast table while I'm trying to read the real news. If I hear one more time how wise and funny and perfect you are, I'm going to suggest she come find you and check out the real thing. I'll tag along just to see the look on her face when she finds out you're as screwed up as the rest of us.

A Non-fan in Reno

Dear Non,

Uncle Mike is sad you woke up on the wrong side of your cage this morning. Sadder still that he is, at least in your little punkin head, responsible for the condition your domestic condition is in. Life can be overwhelming sometimes. Uncle Mike is very sad indeed that your wife reads his column to you while you're trying to read the "real news". Uncle Mike reads the morning paper too, although calling it the real news is something he can no longer manage, and if someone insisted on reading his column out loud, he wouldn't think twice about setting their paper on fire. Now, when they ask why, Uncle Mike can tell them it's a

God on Wheels thing. Thanks for the snappy comeback. On to your real question: is Uncle Mike a boiler plate fraud? Uncle Mike loathes answering questions with questions, but: compared to what? Is Uncle Mike as screwed up as "the rest of us"? He would first need to know, hopefully without actually meeting them, how dysfunctional and whacko you and your us are. As for being wise and funny, qualities which, like beauty and bad slapstick, lie largely in the eye of the beholder, Uncle Mike isn't the person to ask. Like everyone else, Uncle Mike's life has been a carnival of blunders, a tag team wrestling match with the seven deadly sins, an embarrassing pageant of pride and prejudice, a tragic love affair with what mathematical philosophers call the 'error of misplaced concreteness'. It's not called the human comedy for nothing, Cupcake. It only stands to reason that, if you make it to more than seven in dog years (as Uncle Mike has) and you're not dumb as a post (as Uncle Mike isn't), you should have some inkling of what makes the world go round (angular momentum) and a wealth of material to laugh about (the head of Partnership for a Drug Free America spent 12 years as CEO of a major pharmaceutical company). Uncle Mike would consider it a personal favor if neither you nor your lovely wife make him the object of a low rent fact finding mission. Those who have will tell you Uncle Mike's bathrobe isn't up to close scrutiny and his response to visitors who haven't called first often involves answering the door in the nude. And then, what with the change in medication and house training his kangaroo, he's a little too busy for normalcy hearings.

• • •

Dear Uncle Mike,

My mother, God love her, is driving me nuts. She's obsessed with the need for me to be married. I'm a 37 year old man, was married for eight years, have lived alone for five and have no burning desire for a wife. Every time I see her I get the third degree. Am I seeing anyone? What does she do? When am I going to bring her for dinner? I love my mother a lot but it's getting so I dread seeing her. You're the master of snappy one liners. Do you have any that fit this occasion?

Bob W., Eugene, Oregon

Dear Bob,

In Uncle Mike's experience, mothers aren't the best audience for snappy one liners from their grown sons. Your mother is your mother and will manifest her motherliness (or, in her case, motherocity) until one or the other of you croaks. If your mother is one of those who believes her bouncing bumptious boy will never truly be happy until there's some younger version of herself reminding him of his shortcomings and scheduling his activities, there's little to be done but wait. You might try telling her you're single because you've yet to find a woman who can nag as relentlessly as she can. Or you're waiting for someone who shares your budding interest in matricide. As a last resort, for her next birthday, give her a small mallet and a big kiss and tell her that, since she's getting a little dotty, every time she forgets to mind her own business you'll tap her forehead until she comes around. It's the least a son can do.

• • •

Dear Uncle Mike,

At the supermarket the other day, I came close to murder. A woman in the next line spent a good five minutes dealing unsuccessfully with her screaming child. Lord knows what the kid wanted but his mother wasn't giving it. Everyone just tried to ignore it, an impossibility. What do you do in a situation like this?

E.M., Bellevue, Washington

Dear E.M.,

Uncle Mike operates on the premise that it takes a whole village to raise an obnoxious child. Bearing in mind that children these days come with lawyers, if not small automatic weapons, one's approach must be tempered with wisdom, understanding, and a willingness to sacrifice for the long term good of the child. When dealing with budding sociopaths, one needs to strike at the root of the problem. Tell the mother you and every shopper within earshot would be happy to chip in on parenting classes. If your market carries large corks, fetch one and explain its use. In a pinch, a rolled up athletic sock will serve nicely. If these methods fail (and, since the mother is obviously unsuited to raising any creature more challenging than a gerbil, they will), ask permission to speak to the child. Your request will be refused but, since the rules of polite society have already been shredded, feel free to press on. Squat down, put your face six inches from the child's, bore into its little brain with a stare of calm but potentially ugly power, and tell it to shut up. In a country where the child is king, there are no adults.

• • •

Dear Uncle Mike,

I read your column avidly, and your book is never far from my reach. Your truthfulness inclines me to trust you. Here goes. I have decided to end my marriage. The second infidelity and its baggage of lies and lip service are just too much to bear. I am 43 years old and I have a 5 year old daughter with this man I am leaving. I am worried about the effect this divorce will have on her. Any honest wisdom you could toss my way?

Me, Address Withheld

Dear Me,

First off, let Uncle Mike assure you that, whatever ill effects your divorce has on your daughter, they'll be as nothing compared to growing up in a family filled with anger and deceit. There are two aspects to divorce with children: the physical separation of the two halves of the child's whole, and the often insurmountable challenge of single parenting. First, the effects of separation. Regardless how intellectually advanced your daughter is, you mustn't lose sight of the fact that she's five years old and doesn't need a protracted, politically correct explanation for what's happening. Psychobabble in one syllable is till psychobabble. It's enough that she knows her father has things to do that he can't do at home. Come to an agreement with the man to spare your daughter any of the nasty scenes remaining for the two of you to play out. Assure her that her father loves her and isn't leaving her life, and know for yourself it's true. As filled as the world is with ex-husbands, there are no ex-fathers. Unlike your marriage, your daughter has joined the two of you in ways you'll be discovering for many years. More than two parents, your child needs love and

47

security. As she's just discovered, they're not always the same thing. The joy and curse of being a single parent is that one becomes the primary source for both. This doesn't necessarily mean your daughter will suffer the slings and arrows of outrageous misfortune. It means she will have a life different from the one you'd planned for her. This is the way of all children. No endings, no beginnings, only now. For both your sakes, swallow the bitterness and pain. The man you entrusted with your love was too weak and frightened to be honest. No fault, no error, no blame. We're only who we are and, impossible as it sometimes seems, we're all doing the best we can. Be strong, have faith, and never retreat from love.

· · ·

Dear Uncle Mike,

A small problem you'll probably find funny. My boyfriend is an at home nudist. Unless he has to put on clothes, he almost never does. When we were dating, I thought he was cute and sexy, having morning coffee without a stitch on or lolling around in the evening butt naked. Watching him do dishes was a special pleasure. After four months, it's beginning to wear thin. Needless to say we've talked about it. He says he's more comfortable without clothes on and has the right to be comfortable in his own home. I've tried buying him robes, sweat pants, underwear of all shapes, fabrics, styles and colors. He shuns all of them. I'm about to give up. Any suggestions?

Tori S., Portland, Oregon

Dear Tori,

Uncle Mike suggests you give up. Your little wood nymph is absolutely right: barring laws to the contrary (and, so far, there are none governing nakedness in the home), he's allowed to not wear anything he wants. You might remind him he also has the right to live alone. Uncle Mike can only hope for your sake that his appearance flies in the face of the general rule that those most willing to take their clothes off are those who, were witnesses allowed to vote, would be prevented from doing so. This goes a long way toward explaining Uncle Mike's kangaroo pajamas.

• • •

Dear Uncle Mike,

My buddy and I have a bet going. He thinks you're a conservative, I think you're a liberal. We both agree that if we haven't been able to figure you out yet, you're okay either way. Nosey question, right?

Two Guys in Elko

Dear Two Guys,

Nosy seems a bit tame. It's more polite to inquire after someone's intestinal tract than their philosophy of government. But, since you were gauche enough to ask, Uncle Mike is fool enough to answer. If you come upon someone collapsed on the roadside, there are two ways to get them up: lend them a hand or kick them repeatedly. While Uncle Mike is more disposed to the former, he would cheerfully open a major vein before calling himself a liberal; while there are individuals and institutions that cry out more for a boot to the backside than a monthly check, if Uncle Mike and Pat Buchanan were marooned in a cabin, only one would emerge in the spring. Like many of the thoughtful, Uncle Mike gags at a two party system that embodies the democratic principles of Microsoft, Nike, and AT&T but with fewer benefits and less chance for advancement. Politics in the corporate state boils down to a choice between several brands of corn flakes, all of them overpriced and drained of nutritional content. Is Uncle Mike a liberal or a conservative? Yes and no. Given the chance, he'd vote a straight reform ticket since, in his experience, there's precious little about government, and a society that would let it happen, that's not sorely in need of it. As for his religious affiliation, your logical next question, Uncle Mike is a Pythagorean with quantumrelativistic leanings and an abiding love for faeries.

• • •

Dear Uncle Mike,

My boyfriend and I have an ongoing argument about tipping. I say the current rule of fifteen percent is enough, less if the service is mediocre. He never tips less than twenty-five percent and I've seen him leave five dollars on the table to cover two cups of coffee. We both have active professional lives and eat out a great deal. Money's not the issue. Being in business, I just don't believe in paying more than the accepted price for goods and services. We both read your column and would like to know what you think.

Kristin L., Seattle

Dear Kristin,

Uncle Mike thinks you and your boyfriend should find new partners. He could find someone able to distinguish between value and price and you could find someone who had a calculator implanted at birth. Uncle Mike is glad you have an active professional life and hopes it's more pleasant than that of the waiters and waitresses who serve food and beverages to the cheap. It's nice that you eat out a lot. Whenever Uncle Mike does, it's because he's either too lazy to cook or unable to make anything half as good. He tries not to forget that his dining experience involves the short term hiring of personal staff. Yes, your waiter or waitress is paid an hourly wage: one that would nearly cover slamming your plate on the table and ignoring you until you went away. Good service is an art and a vocation. Your tip is an expression of gratitude for being treated like a pasha and respect for anyone who could put up with you and still be gracious. On Uncle Mike's block there are two rules for tipping. If it doesn't fold, it's not a tip, and you could die before you had another chance to treat another human being the way you'd like to be treated. Perhaps your company will downsize and give you the chance to sing for your supper to an audience of the tone deaf. Bon appetit.

• • •

Dear Uncle Mike,

Everywhere I turn, someone is talking about living life "on the edge". I remain unclear why this should be a goal. I am in my midfifties, have been married to the same woman for more than thirty years, and together we have raised three successful children. Neither my wife nor I are dull people. We merely agreed long ago to not take chances whose repercussions would effect the quality of our lives and those of our children. Tell me if I'm wrong, but it seems that living on the edge is a selfish decision that flies in the face of civilization itself and ignores the rewards of a mature, responsible life. Standing on the edge of anything means living constantly in danger of falling. That this seems to be becoming a national spirit is not encouraging.

Centered, Eugene, Oregon

Dear Centered,

Uncle Mike is pleased to hear that you and your wife aren't dull and have raised three successful children. Interesting word, success. While the sort of living on the edge portrayed in commercials for soft drinks and gourmet sneakers appeals to Uncle Mike even less than sliding down a banister lined with broken glass, the idea and the path to fulfillment it represents are part of the human equation. To live on the edge means to be outside, to test the rules in order to see which are grounded in universal truth and which are part of society's shuck and jive machinery of control. All of art and science depend upon questioning what seems to be in light of what is. This includes the art of living a good life and the science of human relationships. Socrates, Einstein, Picasso, and Miles Davis, in showing us their view from the edge, changed the way we perceive the world. One hesitates to call them immature or irresponsible. As Bob Dylan, a child of the middle class, pointed out: to live outside the law you must be honest. To live inside the law, all you need to do is memorize the rules and behave, certain in the knowledge that if you smile and nod enough, master will give you a cookie. Your assumption that this decision is a magic charm against nasty repercussions prompts Uncle Mike to much needed laughter. As someone once suggested, hell is an eternity spent in comfort and certainty. Yes, life on the edge involves the certainty of falling. It also provides humans with their only opportunity to fly. Enjoy your coma.

• • •

Dear Uncle Mike,

I read your column a lot. You don't just make sense, you're funny too. Maybe you can help, or at least make me laugh. My problem is my boyfriend's parents. They have two small dogs. I like dogs okay but these are spoiled rotten and their "parents" make them the center of attention every time we visit. They jump up in my lap every time I sit down. Eating is a nightmare. Unless I feed them bite for bite, I get nasty looks and comments. They even apologize to the dogs for me. Are they nuts or am I? Is there anything I can do to change this situation?

Mary T., Reno

Dear Mary,

Since Uncle Mike doesn't know any of the parties involved, he feels a little squeamish about commenting on their mental condition. This said, you have his sympathies. Is there anything you can do to change the situation? Short of homicide and euthanasia, probably not. Uncle Mike has lived with dogs most of his life and has a profound respect for canine consciousness. He counts his old black lab Easy as one of the great teachers of his life and grieved as much at his passing as he would at the death of family and friends. Never once, however, did he imagine his dog to be at the center of anyone else's universe. Inappropriate behavior is inappropriate behavior, regardless of species. Just as Uncle Mike disapproves of children dominating conversation and behaving as if adults are a combination of captive audience and personal staff, he sees no justification for inflicting little Pookie on guests who came expecting a visit with humans. When Easy mooched food or sniffed crotches, Easy was told to go lie down. When Easy didn't lie down, Easy went outside. Easy lived with Uncle Mike for thirteen years and these rules didn't seem beyond him. Neither did they lessen the bonds of respect and affection that are, to those who love dogs, water for a thirsty soul. All of which counts for nothing when dealing with the people you describe. Imagining they'll change with time is equal to having faith that, given enough tries, one can strike a match on a wet cake of soap. You must simply accept that the dogs' feelings are more important than your own and that, since you're a guest in their kennel, you must behave. The next time the little barkers leap into your lap and demand tummy rubs, remember this is an obnoxious trick they were trained to perform by people who couldn't care less whether you like it or not and who'll be offended if you don't giggle and coo at their "babies". You have three   options. You can become an accomplished actress. You can find a new boyfriend. Or you can roll over and put your paws in the air. Next time you refuse to give the little brats your last bite of coffee cake, slap yourself gently and say, "Oh dear, I've been a bad human," and go sit on the porch.

. . .

Dear Uncle Mike,
    I'm nine years old. My mom and dad told me to write to you. There's a kid in my class who beats up on everybody. Especially me. I'm scared to go to school some times. Mom and dad want me to talk to the teacher or they will. I don't want to tell on him but I want him to stop beating me up.
                                        Aaron P., Portland, Oregon

Dear Aaron,
    You're in a bad situation and Uncle Mike isn't going to candy coat things. The kid is a bully and that's that. There will be other bullies in your life and you're going to have to find a way of dealing with them. First, try harder to avoid him. Stick close to your friends. (Bullies never pick fights they think they'll lose.) Don't try to talk sense into him. His loneliness and pain and anger will drown out anything you say. Just try to remember he acts the way he does for reasons you'll never know. Although telling your teacher wouldn't make you a snitch, Uncle Mike understands why you wouldn't want to. If this kid continues to make your life miserable, your parents should do something to stop it. That's what parents are for. Good luck, little buddy. Hang in there.

. . .

Dear Uncle Mike,

My girlfriend (sic) dresses like a slob. She's not filthy or anything but she never wears anything but jeans or sweat pants or dresses that don't have any shape. Then she wonders why I look at other women! I've tried buying her stuff but she doesn't wear it. Is there something I can do?

Mark in Astoria, Oregon

Dear Mark,

The nice thing about life is that there's always something you can do. The first thing for you to do is to accept your friend for who she is. If she dresses with an exaggerated lack of caring, she was probably dressed that way when you met her. If so, what's changed is you. It's a strange quirk in human mating that the traits that draw us together, the differences we find so attractive and irresistible, are the very things that eventually grate on our nerves. They don't call it the human comedy for nothing, boobla. Uncle Mike finds your part pretty unfunny. That you can describe the person who, in the normal scheme of things, would be your closest friend as a slob makes Uncle Mike's mind reel with misgivings about the depth of your character. He also wonders about the sort of "stuff" you'd like to dress her in. He doesn't wonder at all, and neither should she, that you look at other women. Tell her for Uncle Mike that it just goes with your territory.

• • •

Dear Uncle Mike,

Unlike many of those who write you, my life isn't riddled with difficulties. My love life is fine, my job is satisfying, I have no problem pets, and I'm not obsessed with the implications of quantum theory. My problem is remembering names. My work involves a good deal of socializing and I'm constantly embarrassed by being unable to recall the names of people I've known, on a casual basis, for some time. I was just wondering if, in your travels, you'd come across some simple way of remembering names. Other people must suffer the same syndrome. Thanks for your time.

B.T., Portland, Oregon

Dear B.T.,

Being obsessed with the implications of quantum theory, Uncle Mike regards time as an illusion of the senses, a figment of our measured observation of a seamless everywhere and everywhen. For this reason, and others he'll not go into, Uncle Mike ignores time whenever possible and would open a vein before wearing a personal clock, unless it weighed forty or fifty pounds and was shackled to his neck. He could get behind that as a form of meditation. But you're welcome anyway. Uncle Mike is happy as a bunny to hear your life is going well, aside from your brain's inability to store important information, which is probably nothing to worry about. Uncle Mike has trouble remembering names too. Of course, Uncle Mike has trouble remembering many things. Try this. Since your love life is so grand, try never to go anywhere socially without your partner. Ask her, as a favor, to introduce herself if you don't do so immediately upon meeting another mysterious someone. Done smoothly, they'll never catch on that your neural software has classified them as forgettable. Uncle Mike skated by on this one for years. One small word of warning. It's important that you not have quarreled with your accomplice on the way to the gathering. You don't want to see the way she'll smile and cock an eyebrow as the painful silence falls.

• • •

Dear Uncle Mike,

The other day I was standing outside of a shop, having a smoke while my friend finished his business. A woman walked by on the sidewalk with her daughter, who looked to be about seven. As I usually do, I smiled and nodded. The woman looked at me like I was carrying an ax and told her daughter to hold her breath. I regard myself as a considerate smoker and have no quarrel with rules banning smoking in enclosed public places, but I don't enjoy or believe I deserve being treated like a pariah for engaging in what is, when I last looked, a legal activity. I'm a long time reader and know that you smoke, or at least did, and would appreciate it if you'd answer this in your column. Not so I can see my gripes in print but that it might encourage nonsmokers to loosen the screws a little. Am I expecting too much?

Angela W., Elko, Nevada

55

Dear Angela,

In a word, yes. The health and fitness enlightenment that's somehow generated the most overweight American population in history may sanction dosing their emotionally neglected children with Prozac but they'll never stop flogging you for smoking tobacco anywhere near them. It does no good to remind them that the cars driving past them on the sidewalk belch, annually, their curb weight in known carcinogens and toxic gases vile and various. You will still be, in their mind, a filthy addict whose habit is the greatest threat they face in the pursuit of their bliss. You must remind yourself often that this is their problem. As Socrates probably said, prigs are prigs. As others are born to dance, prigs are born to wretch at the sight of any behavior other than their own. Allow Uncle Mike to share his favorite smoking story. It comes from the late Father Abbot, founder of William Temple House in Portland, and the finest practicing Christian Uncle Mike's ever met. Father Abbot was a Falstaffian figure, full of laughter and life, much loved and respected by everyone who so much as met him, a man who loved good food only slightly more than he loved shopping for it. In the days when smoking was allowed in supermarkets, Father Abbot was standing at the end of the aisle, studying his want list and carefully flicking his ashes into the ashtray provided when an angry dowager stomped to within eight inches of his face. She demanded to know how he, a man of the cloth, could indulge such a filthy habit in public. Father Abbot thought for a moment and answered, "It helps me to mind my own business." That was, of course, then and this is an increasingly ugly and self-righteous now. Good luck. See you on the reservation.

• • •

Dear Uncle Mike,

Why is it that people assume a) their voice is good enough to perform in public, and b) that you want to listen to them sing while you're standing in line at the grocery store? Short of asking them to shut up, what do you do?

D. L., Lincoln City, Oregon

Dear D.L.,

You didn't mention the option of striking their forehead with a small mallet. Uncle Mike respects your restraint. You might try handing them a dollar and telling them you hope their career is more successful than appears likely.

. . .

Dear Uncle Mike,

When I got married a year ago, I thought I'd died and gone to heaven. My wife was all over me. We had sex at least six nights a week, a little less during her cycle. I'd listen to the guys at work with their tales of woe about goings weeks without sex, partners who just laid there, nothing inventive or exciting going on, and I'd smile at how lucky I was, go home and have great sex. Now, I know what they were talking about. If we do it three times a week, I count myself lucky. She's got a new job and says she's just too tired at night. She works late a lot and I'm wondering if she's carrying on with someone at the plant. I haven't changed, she has. She reads your column and maybe if you said something she'd think about it. Other women are starting to look pretty good.

Neglected, Newport, Oregon

Dear Neglected,

With all due respect, Uncle Mike feels it's you who'd benefit from a session with Mr. Thinking Cap. So you had great jungle sex for the first year of your marriage. Good for you. It's a memory you can cherish, along with millions of other men. You mention nothing about your emotional relationship with your wife, a lapse Uncle Mike finds interesting. There's an old and not too pretty truth about the human comedy: women trade sex for love, men trade love for sex. There's a good chance boobla that, after a year of exchanges with you, your wife failed to see the return she was hoping for. This could be because she was expecting too much (yes, ladies, this can happen) or that you delivered too little. Because your concerns are with sex rather than lovemaking (activities as different as masturbation and "great sex"), Uncle Mike suspects you might be the root of your problem. This is a good

57

thing since changing our own behavior is much easier than changing anyone else's. You say you haven't changed. This isn't necessarily something you should be proud of. Those not busy being born are busy dying. Marriages, like the friendships they'd better be, are epics; sagas that make crossing the plains in a covered wagon seem like a much needed vacation. All things change. The corollary to this is that all things better learn to adjust. In simplest terms, you're telling Uncle Mike that your honeymoon is over. Uncle Mike can live with that. So your wife has a new job. Good for her. Uncle Mike hopes it's not one of those that suck your human juices until there's nothing left for yourself and the people you love. Sometimes, money just costs too much. In any case, what the woman needs is your support, not your whiney sexual demands. Uncle Mike recommends you sit down and remind yourself what you love about your wife. What it was, before the naked romps began, that drew you like a ball bearing to a magnet. This done, make a list of all the times she's put your needs ahead of hers, the compromises she's made to please you. You should, by this time, feel like an ungrateful shmuck. Tap your forehead lightly with a mallet and begin your courtship again. This time, as a friend. The secret is to repeat this process every day. As for looking at other women. Other women always look good, cupcake. That's what makes them other women. Living up to your vows is what makes a love affair a marriage.

• • •

Dear Uncle Mike,

My fourteen year old daughter has started listening to rap music. Tell me I shouldn't put her in a box and leave her on the steps of a church.

Mommie Dearest, Portland, Oregon

Dear Mommie,

Okay, you shouldn't put your daughter in a box and leave her on the steps of a church. Most of them are only open on Sunday and she'd just get picked up for vagrancy which would do nothing to make your problem go away. Uncle Mike would like to say everything will work out fine; that your daughter will discover Mozart, learn to clean her room, and marry a surprisingly normal orthodontist. But Uncle Mike must live with himself. Aside from its legendary lyrical preoccupation with hatred, violence and the sexual subjugation of women, rap music is, as a rule of its form, confrontational. To rap means to go on at great length while everyone else shuts up. (See also: skreed.) To rap is to tell, loudly and with self-righteous menace, where you're coming from. Like musical forms whose practitioners bite the heads off rats, rap comes from a place that would, given a society designed for the flowering of human potential, become an embarrassing memory. Yes, they said that about Jerry Lee Lewis. No, it's not the same. Uncle Mike is willing, nay eager, to admit he's a dinosaur who scarcely inhabits the same universe as a fourteen year old with earphones listening to violent felons posture self-indulgent blank verse. If your daughter were his daughter, Uncle Mike would sit on the steps of a church until someone listening to Dr. Dre came by and set fire to him.

• • •

Dear Uncle Mike,

I've never written to an advice column before but you make more sense than most of them so here goes. I'm 20, my boyfriend is 23. We've been together for almost a year and just moved in together two months ago. While we were dating, we were both free to see other people. He did, I didn't, except for a movie once and a dinner. It was hard for me to understand when he saw other women but we're both young and I love 'Jim' a lot. I thought that in time he'd want a monogamous relationship. When we moved in together, we made the same deal. Domesticity being what it is, I have no time for seeing anyone and haven't wanted to anyway. He didn't either until two weeks ago. There's a woman he met a work that 'interests' him. They've had lunch and drinks after work three times and 'Jim' still finds her 'interesting'. I feel real let down. He says he'll let me know if they have sex (honesty is part of our agreement). He knows how I feel but he says he's living up to our agreement and I'm not. He loves me but says he's not ready to limit his friendships with women to just me. I thought I could handle this. Now I'm not sure. I've read your column for a year now, both of us do, and you've given other people good advice. I hope you have some for me. Please don't print my address, it's a pretty small town and some of our friends read your column too.

'Cindy', Somewhere in Oregon

Dear 'Cindy',

Uncle Mike has advice for everyone. That's why he's Uncle Mike. It's also why many people avoid him. It sounds like you and 'Jim' need to renegotiate. While Uncle Mike can understand, in theory, an open dating relationship, he has yet to see a successful marriage between cohabitation and free love. Uncle Mike can scarcely imagine how lucky 'Jim' must have felt when you agreed to an arrangement that satisfies his rambunctious needs at the cost of tearing your heart, and your guts, out. If you've made your feelings plain, you must assume he's doing the same. He's decided his sexual freedom is more important than your emotional balance. Fair enough. The long wait is over, you finally know who, or what, you're dealing with: someone lame enough to bite the hand that feeds it and, Uncle Mike would bet his dear mother's pension, also does its laundry and dirty dishes. 'Jim' Bob is right. It's he who's honoring your agreement. One would be hard pressed to find a reason he wouldn't. Given your feelings, one would be harder pressed to find a reason you would. Trust Uncle Mike, given the situation you describe, love isn't enough. It's not even in shouting distance. Unless one of you changes your position, freely and in good spirit, you can't continue to do emotional business together. Congratulations. You've learned something about yourself you didn't know before. Thank your friend for the teaching and move on to someone whose sensitivity and compassion are greater than the average reptile.

• • •

Dear Uncle Mike,

Is there a right and wrong way to eat spaghetti?

Alan C., Portland, Oregon

Dear Alan,

Probably.

・・・

Dear Uncle Mike,

Can you answer me a question? Why is it that girls dress provocatively and then get upset when you look at them? Don't they know guys see this as teasing? I think it's two-faced to dress to get attention and then gripe about being considered a sex object. What do you think?

Pete in Seattle

Dear Pete,

Uncle Mike thinks you're young and that the world has much to teach you. The safest assumption you can make is that girls, and women, dress the way they do because it pleases them to do so. It may be that they're proud of their bodies. It might be that, like many humans, they hunger for any attention they can get. It could even be that, being smarter than a two by four, they've learned that men can't always be depended upon to be attracted to a good mind. After years of observation, Uncle Mike thinks women get upset only if the wrong men look at them. Or if a right one does it the wrong way. Or if they're not in the mood to be looked at by anyone, especially someone who's obviously mistaking them for a steak. Do they see this as teasing? No, they see it as trolling. How you and the other fish see it is, quite correctly, none of their concern. Men are attracted to beauty, women are attracted to power. Uncle Mike hopes you never inflate your resume to some sweet young thing only to find you've become a success object.

・・・

Dear Uncle Mike,

Some friends were over last week and the conversation turned to marriage. Is it dead or dying? A relic of a male dominated culture? The glue that holds society together or the outdated response to survival conditions that no longer exist? Aside from child rearing, does it have a place in modern society? We'd be interested in your thoughts.

Four Couples in Portland

Dear Potential Family Units,

Does marriage have a place in modern society? Only if humans do. Any media traumatized, self centered upright hominid with its mentalemotional baseball cap turned backwards can fall in love. It takes a full blown human (or the average member of several 'lesser' species) to pair bond for life. Uncle Mike has no idea what goes on between mated wolves and geese but with humans marriage involves a vow, an ancient term for which 'promise' is a puny reflection. A vow is a pledge made, not just between two people, but between those people and whatever it is they perceive to be powers larger and greater than themselves. Vows, to use another outdated term, are holy bonds, dissolved only by death. This is a tough gig to pitch in a world where 'relationships' have the shelf life of disposable razors. The notion of keeping your word and rising to the challenge of building and maintaining a lifelong love between equals sounds pretty silly to those who've been taught that the next relationship is bound to be better, or at least different. Marriage presupposes faith, determination, and the willingness to put someone else before yourself. To honor and cherish that person as if they were a message from the heart of all that is. Is marriage a relic of male domination? If this is a serious question, none of you have seen a good one. Male domination is a relic, marriage is its antimatter. There is, goodness knows, much to be said for the single life; but when practiced overlong, it tends to breed the sort of hollow self indulgence that malls, condominiums, and hundred dollar sneakers were born to feed on. Marriage is the art of complementarity; the affirmation that, while two can't eat as cheaply as one, the food will taste better and be more nourishing. Uncle Mike is a great fan of enduring domestic units whether children are involved or not. Men and women have much to learn from each other and nothing beats studying your whole life with someone who wants you to ace every test.

• • •

Dear Uncle Mike,

My boyfriend and I moved in together a month ago. He has a male sheep dog named Ralph. Is there any way to train a male dog to stop licking its genitals?

Deborah S., San Mateo, California

Dear Deborah,

No there's not. Beating poor Ralph with a rolled up newspaper will only turn him into a sneak. Lest you regard his pursuit of personal bliss as another example of what one can expect of males in general, Uncle Mike would remind you that the girls of dogdom are every bit as self serving. This isn't to say you should give up trying. Go on throwing your boot at the old pervert. If nothing else, it'll help relieve your tensions.

. . .

Dear Uncle Mike,

I know writing to you will help about as much as writing to Santa Claus, but I need to let off steam. And my girlfriend reads your column so what the hell. Whenever she goes shopping for clothes, I have to go along. She says it's something we can do together and she needs my opinion. If I had a nickel for every time she followed my advice, I'd have a dime. What it amounts to is me following her like a little boy up and down the aisles, holding skirts and blouses and being bored out of my skull. Sitting down in the little chairs to wait is worse. It's like being in detention. I've told her how much I hate it but she starts pouting and says she doesn't ask much (yeah right) and if I really loved her and blah blah blah. Got any silver bullets for this one, Uncle Mike?

Don't Use My Name, Beaverton, Oregon

Dear Don't,

If Uncle Mike did have a silver bullet, he's afraid what he might do with it. You might not be old enough to understand, but there are things in life we do, not because we want to, but because it makes someone else happy. Not being Santa Claus, Uncle Mike

63

has no illusions this revelation will change your life. He does have two suggestions. Next time you go to the skateboard shop, insist she come along. Or get out a long sheet of paper and list the things the poor woman does to keep you from pouting and holding your breath.

• • •

Dear Uncle Mike,

I think I need some advice. There's a young woman I've known for about a year now. We met through a mutual friend and hit it off right away. We both work down town and meet for lunch or after work at least once a week and talk on the phone regularly. The whole time I've known her, she's had a boyfriend. I was seeing someone at first but haven't had a 'relationship' for several months now. I'm 32 by the way and she's 26, if that makes any difference. I've always had feelings for her but have always bitten my tongue, even when she's been quarreling with her boyfriend and comes over to my apartment at midnight crying. We've become close friends and I think she values me as much as I value her. Last week, her boyfriend broke up with her. I think she's better off without him, in a way she does too, but they've been together for two years and she's understandably hurt and lonely. You've probably guessed my question. Should I tell her how I feel? She's pretty vulnerable and I'm not sure now's the time but I'm afraid if I don't somebody else will. She's very good looking, really smart, and a good person. I personally know three guys who are interested. I don't want to blow our friendship but I don't want to miss my chance either. If you were me, what would you do?

C.D., Bend, Oregon

Dear C.D.,

If Uncle Mike were in your position, something far more likely and much different than ever actually being you, he'd probably put first priority on maintaining the friendship. This doesn't mean he wouldn't tell the young woman how he felt; only that, before he did, he'd have vowed to himself not to behave like someone in a bad sitcom if her response fell somewhere between a gentle no and nervous laughter. She obviously trusts you with her emotions, at least the ones involving tears at midnight. This is a good thing. You don't mention any new signals of interest from her. This could mean she's still in mourning. It could also mean she has none. In Uncle Mike's experience, much of it too humiliating for words, if a woman wants you, she'll find a way to let you know.

. . .

Dear Uncle Mike,

Does it strike you as a little bit odd that, during two terms of a Democratic presidency, corporate profits have created thousands of new millionaires and increased the gap between the rich and the working class?

Benjamin D., Seattle

Dear Ben,

Nothing about politics strikes Uncle Mike as the slightest bit odd; certainly not that the people who make the laws make laws that further their own interests and the interests of those with whom they golf. Political affiliation aside, fat cats feed themselves first and make speeches about free enterprise and school vouchers to people whose portion of the level playing field is a strip mine. Uncle Mike finds nothing odd about greed, self-righteousness, and self indulgence in history's first experiment with government by global corporation. An old story comes to mind. A traveler goes to the end of the world and finds a huge beast eating the planet so fast it barely has time to swallow. The traveler asks the beast why he's eating everything. "Because I can," it answers. But why, when there's clearly enough to go around, is he eating it so fast? "Because," the beast says between bites, "one day it will all be gone."

. . .

Dear Uncle Mike,

I think I need some advice. I'm a 26 year old married woman. My husband owns his own business and works long hours and most weekends. I love him very much but his schedule leaves little time for the two of us. I knew this when we got married a year ago but I guess I underestimated its effects on me. There's only so much I can do around the house so to fill my time and keep from going stir crazy, I enrolled in classes at the local community college. There's a guy in my poetry class who's invited me several times to have coffee with him. He's a nice person and I'm pretty sure his invitation is innocent. He knows I'm married. Although he's attractive and the sort of person who, if I were single, I'd be interested in, I'm just looking for someone to talk to about literature and ideas. My best friend says there's nothing wrong with having a cup of coffee after class. I haven't talked about it with my husband because there's nothing to talk about and I think he might misunderstand. I'd like to get to know this person better, I think he could be a real friend, and I'm definitely not looking for an affair. Does meeting a classmate for coffee without my husband knowing qualify as being unfaithful? Should I or shouldn't I?

"Emily", Portland

Dear Emily,

As innocent as you make everyone out to be, Uncle Mike smells trouble. Having been a young man himself once, he knows all about poetry classes and the sort of emotional intoxication that arises from group groping great ideas. He also knows a thing or two about young men. More than enough, since there are only one or two things you need to know about them. Unless you spent your premarital years trapped in a cave, you know that young men's most fervent desire, after understanding what T.S. Eliot was really saying, is to get laid. Your young man may not be like this. He could also be from another planet. As for you, young lady, Uncle Mike thinks you may be protesting too much. Uncle Mike fears that, underneath the iambic pentameter, you're a bored young housewife looking to fill a hollowness in her life. It's not nice to involve others in your search for fulfillment through distraction. Giving you the benefit of overwhelming doubt, let's say your interests are purely platonic, that your hormones aren't cranking out bad sonnets and your behavior toward this person has never once been flirtatious, even in the Elizabethan sense. You could be from another planet too. If what you're looking for is a meeting of the minds, the more the merrier. Say yes to the coffee and invite at least one other person in your class to join you and Lancelot. Good sense dictates the person should be female. Then, when your husband, old What's His Name who's working his hindquarters off building what Uncle Mike can only think was a mutually agreed upon future, asks about your day, you can tell him the unedited truth.

• • •

Dear Uncle Mike,
    My girlfriends and I think you rock hard. Extra special cool. We want to marry you and have your babies. Interested?
                                        Three Fans in Eugene, Oregon

Dear Mouseketeers,
    Uncle Mike bursts with pride to know you find his rocking cool. However, as much as his heart goes pitter-pat at the way you dot your i's with little circles, he must turn down your generous offer of polygamy. His therapy group thinks it would only lead to more trouble.

• • •

Dear Uncle Mike,
    I hope you can help me make a big decision. I'm sixteen and my boyfriend is too. He wants to have sex but I'm not sure. We've sort of had sex but not really, if you know what I mean. We've been going together for six months and I love him and he says he loves me. One of my friends says I should and the other one says I shouldn't. I want to but I just don't know. I don't want to lose him. Do you think I should? Don't print my name okay?
                                        Name Withheld, Elko, Nevada

Dear Anonymous,

Uncle Mike suggests you wait. Sex is much more than a delicious joining of body parts. It's an electromagnetic, biochemical merging of two souls. Given the right spirit on the part of both, it's a religious experience: the marriage of difference to produce a whole greater than the sum of its naughty bits. Done lightly (see: recreational sex), it's a short circuit that, while too exciting for words, can burn up a person's emotional wiring. There was an interesting study done a while back on American youth. (Uncle Mike gags at the term 'teenager'.) Sexually active young men have a better self image than their frustrated male friends, while sexually active young women have a lower self image than those who've managed to keep the wolves at bay. There are several messages here. Your boyfriend's expectations of sex will be fulfilled by the act. Your expectations will be awakened by it. What makes him feel like a physical success may make you feel like an emotional failure. Unless you truly believe you and your young man are prepared to create an extraordinarily complex bond involving, not just healthy lust, but loyalty and the sort of compassion most adults have difficulty maintaining, Uncle Mike suggests the two of you keep your bloomers on. As for losing him, relax my young friend. You never lose anything you can't do without. And you can always tell what's really yours by whether it's there or not.

• • •

Dear Sir:

I am sure you expected some flak about your comments on obesity. I couldn't help being predictable and taking offense. While I agree we are a country of couch potatoes, there are many out there who have emotional problems that lead to eating disorders that are comparable to other mental disorders and addictions. May I point out that people with weight problems are not all dull-witted sloths? Many are discriminated against based on their physical appearance. An alcoholic can get and hold a job and may not be suspected as having a problem but many overweight people can't even land the job because of the prejudice we have towards them.

Just because obese people wear their addictions on the outside, insensitive boobs, such as yourself, feel it's OK to make fun of them. Many women live their lives feeling inferior because they do not measure up to a totally unrealistic "thin" image they are convinced they should achieve.

Yellow Bellied Fat Cow, Portland

Dear Yellow,

Uncle Mike can't help being taken aback. After shuffling repeatedly through his back files, the only letter he found which made any reference to obesity was in answer to a woman in Nevada who'd been treated like a dangerous leper for smoking a cigarette on the sidewalk. Uncle Mike responded with this: "The health and fitness enlightenment that's somehow generated the most overweight American population in history may sanction dosing their emotionally neglected children with Prozac but they'll never stop flogging you for smoking tobacco anywhere near them." If you consider this an attack on overweight people, Uncle Mike must make two assumptions: 1) that you're a little too tightly wrapped, and 2) you've never read his column before and hence have no notion of how vicious and petty he can be. Now then, on to you and the points you make so pugnaciously. Is Uncle Mike aware of an emotional basis for eating disorders? You bet. That these disorders are comparable to other mental disorders and addictions? Absolutely. He's also aware of the sort of genetic predisposition that produces sumo wrestlers. To this, Uncle Mike would only reply that we all have our crosses to bear and demons to fight. It's nice that people like you are there to steadfastly defend those addicted to tobacco, strong drink, and controlled substances. You do, right? Uncle Mike cannot remember ever thinking, let alone saying, that overweight people are "all dull-witted sloths". In the first place, he's not convinced that sloths are dull-witted, certainly no more than the legions of sleek and clueless who jog in hundred dollar sneakers and deep breathe exhaust fumes. You mention that many of the overly plump are discriminated against because of their physical appearance. Imagine that, a less than perfect world in which surface is rewarded more than substance. Maybe all of those black people were right. Discrimination in hiring based on percentage of body fat? The folks you want to talk to are the insurance companies who feel, along with the folks in health sciences, that, since obesity is a prime factor in heart disease and stroke as well as a strong contributor to other maladies vile and various, it constitutes a personal as well as a national health problem. "Just because obese people wear their addictions on the outside, insensitive boobs, such as yourself, feel it's OK to make fun of them." Innocent. Uncle Mike has his hands full poking fun at insensitive boobs. As for the many women who "live their lives feeling inferior because they do not measure up to a totally unrealistic 'thin' image they are convinced they should achieve", Uncle Mike feels much compassion for them and sincerely hopes they grow a brain. Buying into hogwash is a personal choice. Much like that second trip to the buffet.

• • •

Dear Uncle Mike,
       When you take a girl to a restaurant and they take you to the table, does the guy go first or the girl?
                              Eric S., Astoria

Dear Eric,
       Uncle Mike is surprised that, living in Astoria, the question ever came up. Like most matters of etiquette, it depends. As a rule of thumb, the young lady is deferred to and precedes her escort to the table. This doesn't apply if the joint to which you've taken her is known for impromptu apache dancing and the breaking of beer pitchers over heads. In this case, neither of you should go first. Before you ask, it's the gentleman's responsibility to pass judgment on the wine. This is so the lady doesn't cut her nose sniffing the screw cap.

• • •

Dear Uncle Mike,

My boyfriend and I are very physical. We wrestle around a lot. Sometimes he lets me win. It's a lot of fun and sexy. We usually have great sex afterwards. Except when he tickles me. I've told him I don't like it but he just laughs. We've had fights about it (not physical) but he still does it sometimes. Is there any way to get him to stop?

Kate in Seattle

Dear Kate,

Uncle Mike would like to suggest tapping his forehead lightly with a mallet; but since the first rule on the playground is that nobody hits anyone ever, he won't. Uncle Mike sees two possible approaches. The first involves waiting around for the nimrod to start taking you seriously as a human and respect your wishes. The second is to cut your losses and find someone who knows how to play nice. Speaking of play, the sort you're indulging in would be seen by an alien naturalist as a ritualized power struggle whose object is domination and submission, faux warfare different only in degree from boxing and football. Relationships aren't sports and domination is for sissies.

• • •

Dear Uncle Mike,

I'm a thirty-eight year old executive in a small corporation. Aside from an unsuccessful marriage of twelve years, I have nothing to complain about. I do, however, have a dilemma. I've worked closely for more than a year with a young woman in the office. My interests are becoming more than professional. I may be reading too much into small gestures, but she seems to find me attractive. There are two problems. First, that I'm married. Divorce would be possible, but messy, angry, and expensive. Second, the gender politics of the workplace. Although Miss X doesn't work for me, my position in the company is higher than hers. I'm not the type to harass anyone, male or female, but I worry that personalizing the relationship would make her feel

71

uncomfortable, even though she knows I'm married and she doesn't have a boyfriend. I don't personally read your column but a good friend suggested I write and get your perspective. In my position, what would you do?

Name Withheld, Lake Oswego, Oregon

Dear Bored and Oblivious,

In your position, Uncle Mike would get a divorce, a course he suspects would leave your wife a happier woman. You're right to suspect you might be reading more into small gestures than are really there. Men like you usually do. You'll save everyone a lot of trouble if you stop reading them at all. Any man with a conscience more evolved than a rattlesnake would leave young Miss X (cute name, by the way) alone. Since this probably doesn't apply to you, by all means ask her out some evening you're not expected home for dinner. If she says yes, she's the girl for you. Uncle Mike wishes you happiness and fulfillment, and only hopes you apply a finer sense of ethics to your business dealings than the smarmy ones you foist onto those closest to you.

• • •

Dear Uncle Mike,

You keep saying you don't know anything about etiquette but you've given some pretty good answers before and you have to know more about it than me since I'm only 17. I've always eaten with the fork in my right hand. I see a lot of people now eating with the fork in the left hand and the knife in the right. It looks cool but is it etiquette?

Chris, Yachats, Oregon

Dear Chris,

First off, there's no such thing as only seventeen. By then, Mozart had been composing for ten years and Einstein had been passed over in mathematics. But your question involves knives and forks. We push on. Uncle Mike isn't just pretending to know nothing about etiquette. Aside from common manners, which chimpanzees are more than capable of mastering, Uncle Mike would be regarded by members of court as either, depending upon the gaucherie involved, an amusing bumpkin or a well meaning savage. You have, perhaps without knowing, hit upon the first rule of etiquette: it must, to outsiders, look cool. The second rule is that the more complex and arbitrary the anointed behavior, the better the form. There must be a third rule, but Uncle Mike would hate to guess what it is. Neither is he curious. Uncle Mike holds his fork in his left hand, pointy ends down. This leaves his right hand free to make conversational points with his knife. It also conserves energy. When Uncle Mike thinks of the cumulative hours he's spent cutting his food into manageable portions, laying down the knife and transferring the fork to his right hand before lobbing his bite in the general direction of his mouth, he could just slap his forehead and make cuckoo sounds. Aside from the lobbing part, this, the European method, is considered the proper use of the knife and fork in every civilized country but this one. From what Uncle Mike has seen, you're perfectly free to follow either form. The way you do it just isn't as cool.

• • •

Dear Uncle Mike,
    Please don't think I'm weird. If I fantasize about someone while I'm having sex with myself, is this psychic molestation?
                    Laurie Elf, Eugene, Oregon

Dear Laurie,
    Anyone whose last name, inherited or adopted, is Elf shouldn't have to ask. Repeat after Uncle Mike: All things are one thing. That's why we call it a universe, from the Latin, "entire, whole". The ultimate unity of objects and events is not just a linguistic convention, it is a description of a quantum reality predicted by equations and borne out by observation. In the world behind this one, where quantum relativity dances with the faerie faith, there is no distinction between one thing and another; no this and that, no here or there, no thee and me. There is only a sea of unmanifest possibility rippled by the winds of spacetime: a dazzling illusion,

73

which, many physicists believe, is a product of a universal consciousness. In this view, you and Uncle Mike are point conscious perspectives, creating what is from what might be, at play in the fields of spacetime. You chose your last name well. Are you psychically molesting the object of your sexual fantasies? Like everything else, it depends on your attitude. You're generating ripples in the pond that are felt everywhere in the creation. That you're addressing these ripples to your object's quantum e-mail could presumably focus their effects. Uncle Mike would suggest you make love not just to yourself, but to him or her. As any elf will tell you, the secret is to love people and use things. As a quantum elf would tell you, the distinction between people and things is an illusion.

· · ·

Dear Uncle Mike,

Great column. Good advice. I noticed a letter to you from Elko recently from a 16 year old girl asking if she should give in to her boyfriend's sexual demands. I thought your advice was sound; I just hope she understood it. That's what most kids around here worry about it seems. I remember kids dating (and more, according to rumor), but the kids I have in class (I teach English in Elko) are considered losers if they're not going out with someone or they don't get drunk, etc. Oh, sure, we have our fair share of good, hard working kids, but the social element is out of whack. It's almost like a college "social life" atmosphere here. Did I miss something? When did sex, drugs, and rap begin to be the ultimate concerns? Probably a very long time ago, I know. I guess I just fear for these kids. They expect everybody to take care of them— teachers, parents, etc. When they wake up one day and nobody can help them, what will they do? Mike, any advice? I'd like to be able to focus them a little. By the way, I use your article in class on occasion for journal topics. I find it interesting that the advice you gave for the person standing in line behind a want-to-be singer was to be rude and embarrassing. However, when a gal from Elko wrote in to say that smokers are treated like lepers, you answered that people are jerks and they should let people smoke. So, people can pollute my lungs, and I should be tolerant, but if a person is singing I should give them a dollar and recommend more lessons? I'm sorry, Mike, I can't follow the logic. Thanks for your time. If you have any advice for me and my sex-crazed students, I would welcome it.

David Hayes, Elko, Nevada

Dear Dave,

Thanks for writing. It's good to hear from someone in the trenches of public education, even if the news is less than upbeat. Your concern for your students is not only cause for hope but also gives Uncle Mike an excuse to lash out at a culture, ours, that's degenerating into a cheesy lifestyle we're foisting off on our children. Let's talk about television, shall we? When Uncle Mike was a young person, television was a young medium. People watched it the way they watched movies: as entertainment. While young Uncle Mike watched Zorro and Robin Hood, he never once imagined he should wear a mask or make his mark in the world by shooting burning arrows into castles. One watched television; one didn't imitate it. Two generations later, reality is determined by whether or not it looks like something we've seen on cable. Human behavior is being radically altered by people, the networks and their corporate sponsors, whose only motivation is to sell us something. To sell something for which there is no clear need (amazing new advances in toothpaste, pain relief, minivans, and feminine hygiene), one must first generate dissatisfaction. The more general the level of dissatisfaction, the broader the array of useless garbage that can be sold. The mother of all garbage is that set of behaviors and attitudes one used to see only in television commercials: mindless consumption, smug self-righteousness, disrespect of values other than your own, and an imagined right to instant gratification. Add to this mix that truly American invention, the marriage of sex and violence, and you have not only the perfect sitcom but also the perfect consumer: insecure, frightened, and titillated, ready to buy or do anything that makes it feel better. And we wonder who's minding the children. As for Uncle Mike's recommendations for dealing with outdoor smokers and indoor, unrequested vocals, he stands pat.

• • •

Dear Uncle Mike,

When encountering smokers, I suggest striking their forehead with a small mallet, since it's not half as cute as singing in public.

Jennifer Dixon, Portland

Dear Jennifer,

Like beauty, cuteness lies in the ear of the beholder. To Uncle Mike, involuntarily listening to someone whose theatrical vibrato is more developed than their ability to select tones launch into selections from Evita is about as uncute as life gets. But, since Uncle Mike is against violence even with small mallets, he suggests asking the singer if he or she takes requests. If they answer yes, ask them to mime the libretto from Oh, Calcutta.

• • •

Dear Uncle Mike,

My husband's sister has invited the family to Thanksgiving dinner at her house. The family is a large one and dinner will be for fourteen. There are several children, one of them our eight year old daughter. The hostess has arranged a separate table for the children and now I'm not sure I want to go. I see no reason that children cannot be integrated with adults, especially at Thanksgiving. My husband says we should go along, there's no harm in letting the children eat at the next table, that they might even enjoy it. I've never heard of it. Your opinion, please?

Traditional in Eugene, Oregon

Dear Traditional,

The opinion Uncle Mike would like to hear is your daughter's. While Uncle Mike is a staunch advocate of including children in nearly everything (they certainly should not be deprived of a chance to see how weird Aunt Mable can really be), unless their table is in a separate building, he doesn't see your sister-in-laws seating arrangement as an assault on their holiday rights. Not only does it preclude much boredom on their part with the state of Cousin

Ralph's gall bladder surgery or how much Uncle Dweeb spent on his vacation to Mossy Rock, and the inevitable urge to do something to attract attention, it gives the young people a chance to share table conversation with their family peers. By the time they're the Aunt Mables and Uncle Dweebs, your daughter will have much ammunition.

• • •

Dear Uncle Mike,

My girlfriend and I both have very demanding jobs and rarely go out to eat, preferring to spend evenings at home unwinding from the day. We do have a Sunday ritual. We get up about nine, buy a Sunday paper and go to a diner in the neighborhood for breakfast. Simple pleasures. Last week, it was a nightmare. A couple with two small children sat down at the table behind us. Even by today's standards, the children were unbelievable. They argued and fussed, were rude to their parents and sullen with the waitress, monopolized the conversation in voices that would carry on a playground, were granted all wishes from the menu and then refused to eat the food when it came. The entire time, the parents behaved like servants, occasionally asking the children to not do something and doing nothing when their whiny requests were ignored. This lasted for nearly an hour and entirely ruined our morning. I know you can't do anything about it but dammit I felt like complaining to someone and you're it. I'm supposed to feel better now but I don't.

David in Portland

Dear Dave,

Uncle Mike is sorry you don't feel better. Neither does he. On bad days, he harbors much resentment at a universe that put him on the planet with twenty-foot underwater snakes and small humans who, as opposed to being raised, are allowed merely to get larger. He can get a little whiny himself. Uncle Mike has spent much time brooding over the collapse of civilized behavior and, small surprise to his friends, lays much of the responsibility on television. Back in the Great Repression, before we realized the purpose of adults was to cater to children, the task of transmitting cultural values to young hominids was divided between the school and the family, social structures whose goals were to produce reasonably competent human beings. We've since contracted the service out to corporate media; business structures whose goals are to sell us something. Since children are the easiest to pander to, and because they can, by being relentlessly obnoxious, wear down the sturdiest of wimpy parents who believe their willingness to surrender to their children makes them facilitators of their bliss, there are now several hundred sorts of frosted cereal, several thousand lines of unimaginative toys, and several million pairs of hundred dollar tennis shoes in small sizes. And many too many children who behave like child actors. The day after he wins the lottery, Uncle Mike plans to retain a ruthless and long fanged attorney to sue the FCC for allowing children to be portrayed as authority figures whose faux cute search for immediate gratification qualifies them as objects of fear and worship. Regardless what Madison Avenue tells us, children are not small adults, they're apprentice humans. They share with adults certain inalienable rights; not among these are unbridled behavior at the table, rude behavior in public places, disregard of the rights of others, and disrespect of their elders. Say what you will about repressive child rearing, Uncle Mike would much rather dine with the Cleaver children than with Beavis and Butthead. All of which is Uncle Mike's way of saying that, unless you're Chairman of the FCC, own at least one major network, or are crowned absolute monarch, there's not much you can do to alter the behavior of other people's children. In the situation you described, one with which Uncle Mike is all too familiar, he's had some success with the half-glare. When the little whelps' volume reaches levels that qualify as noise pollution, Uncle Mike swivels half way round on his stool, examines the tableau with the dispassionate interest of an anthropologist who's stumbled onto something he'd hoped was extinct, sighs heavily and shakes his head. He finds this works best when he avoids eye contact with the parents. Not out of cowardice, but to save them the embarrassment of defending their indefensible offspring and their woeful abilities as parents. If the chance presents itself, Uncle Mike isn't above fixing small tyrants with a look that reminds them they're puppies among big dogs. He refuses to see this as child abuse.

• • •

Dear Uncle Mike,

I read your column religiously and believe you give sound advice. I am a 43 year old professional woman. Recently I met a man whom I really like. The problem is that my occupation requires that I attend a lot of functions both work related and community oriented. Often an escort is a real plus. A friend I met, I will call him "Dave", is very willing to go with me, but I find it difficult to ask him to go. His grammar is very bad, he tries to use words that he does not know how to use in order to impress people. He is very hard working, a very gentle person to be around but his lack of the English language is causing a serious problem. Do you have any suggestions?

Professional, Hillsboro, Oregon

Dear Semi-Pro,

Uncle Mike always has suggestions. That's why his circle of friends is so small. What you're wrestling with is another of life's endless lessons in trade-offs. Only in the movies would it be as simple as deciding whose feelings were more important, those of your friend or your those of your obligatory acquaintances. In real life, both are important. Having your gentleman accompany you to social goldfish bowls in which he is neither accomplished nor comfortable does no one any favors and furthers no one's goals. On the other hand, if the social carp assembled can't deal with a good and gentle human being whose vocabulary and grammar don't measure up, they should jolly well learn. The real problem is your embarrassment. This will probably decrease as, or if, his value in your life increases. As for immediate solutions, there really are none. If you don't accept his offers to accompany you, he'll feel bad and you'll feel worse. If you do accept, you'll be nervous and, unless he's more dense than he sounds, he'll know you're ashamed of him. You could, of course, go to fewer schmoozes in order to have more quiet dinners and long walks with someone who's proved his willingness to go through hell and boredom to be with you.

Dear Uncle Mike,

My husband and I have been trying to conceive a child for seven years without success. We would like to have children but will be okay if it doesn't happen. I'm writing because with the holidays coming up, we're sure to get the usual questions about when the grandchildren can be expected. With the recent birth of septuplets, someone is bound to bring up fertility drugs. What are your thoughts on them? After many years of facing the same question, our answers no longer satisfy the family. We thought you might have a ready answer, or at least a humorous response we could use.

Okay With or Without, Lakeview, Oregon

Dear Okay,

Uncle Mike loves a challenge and few compare to coming up with charming, instructive, and self satisfying ways to tell someone to mind their own business. A few suggestions for your inquiring minds. Philosophical: "Like all things, it will happen at just the right moment." Solicitous: "Knowing how oddly anxious you are about it is an inspiration to us." Sly: "Believe me, we're doing everything we can. If you get my meaning." Religious: "Maybe God is punishing you and dad and I'm just the vehicle." Straightforward: "How very tasteless of you to ask." Blunt: "Don't you have affairs of your own to think about?" Uncle Mike sympathizes with your plight. When, if, why or why not any two people do or don't reproduce may be a matter of interest to others, but it is not a proper subject for repeated conversation. Uncle Mike has great faith in the whimsy of natural selection, the law of karma, and the truth that whatever is is right. He applauds your stance that, if you're meant to have children, you will. If not, no fault, no blame. As for fertility drugs, Uncle Mike confesses to serious reservations. In the recent obstetric miracle, the couple were not childless. They merely wanted more. If they were Latino and living in East Los Angeles, the media would have clucked instead of cooed. There's an ugly sense of arrogance involved in practicing overpopulation in a world riddled with poverty and overstocked with unwanted children. Even uglier is when we treat those who do it like they just invented family values.

Dear Uncle Mike,

I want to give my girlfriend something special for Christmas this year. Would you write a love poem for me to give to her? If she sees it in the paper she'd get a big kick out of it and know how much I care about her. She likes your column.

Randolph, Portland P.S. Her name is Susan

Dear Randolph,

At the risk of sounding rude, Uncle Mike must ask if you're taking powerful drugs; and suggest that, if you're not, you might consider it. Let's take things step by step, shall we? You want to give your girlfriend something special for Christmas. That's a good thing. But the something special you want to give her is a love poem Uncle Mike writes. This is dangerously fuzzy thinking. A blender would have more personal meaning. And then you want Uncle Mike to put it in the column so that, when she sees it, she'll be tickled and know how much you care. Randolph, Randolph, Randolph. This could only work if she knew you paid me a large sum of money to publish greeting card copy with her name on it. Before we begin negotiations, you should know Uncle Mike has professional standards and doesn't come cheap. You should also know he stopped writing poetry a quarter century ago out of kindness to his fellow humans. Sorry. Uncle Mike suggests you crib a little Rod McKuen. And put it into the blender.

• • •

Dear Uncle Mike,

Someone recently brought a copy of your book 'Letters to Uncle Mike' into my bar. At first, just a couple of people were reading. Then they started reading out loud and laughing. Pretty soon a small crowd gathered and we were all in tears. Really. We all want to thank you for the laughs and tell you we think you really nail it. If you're ever in Fallon, stop by. The drinks are on the house. (Yes, we have sour mash whiskey.)

Bartender in Fallon, Nevada

Dear Bartender,

Uncle Mike is glad you enjoyed his book. You can't imagine what it means to him to know you folks out there in Fallon are sitting around getting pie eyed and reading his work out loud. It doesn't get much better than that. As soon as he finishes this letter, Uncle Mike plans to call his mother who never lost faith that her boy would someday make good. Thank you too for your gracious invitation. If Uncle Mike ever finds himself in Fallon, he'll doubtlessly need strong drink.

• • •

Dear Uncle Mike,

I've been with my girlfriend for almost a year and she's great. We're great. For the first time in my life, I'm 23, I think I'm starting to realize what love is. So if everything's so great, why am I writing to you? Last week, Mary (not really) dyed her hair blonde. She didn't tell me she was going to do it, I just came home and there she was. It's okay but I liked her better as a brunette. She thinks it's fun and no big deal. I think she might at least have talked it over with me before she made such a big change. She gets a lot more stares now when we go out. She doesn't seem to notice but I sure do. I liked things better the way they were. When I ask if she's going to let it go back, she says she doesn't know and I should stop pouting about it. I say I have a right to my feelings too. Am I making too much of this?

J.K., Seattle, Washington

Dear J.K.,

In a word, yes. The question isn't whether or not you're off base, but which of the bases you're furthest off. Uncle Mike would first like to congratulate you on realizing, at age twenty-three, what love is. To have accomplished this, your emotional IQ must be, not just higher than your age peers, but higher than most of humanity's. When Uncle Mike thinks what it must be like to understand love, he weeps with joy at your achievement. No, Uncle Mike is being sarcastic. He chuckles to think of the lessons awaiting you. So your girlfriend changed her hair color. The nerve.

And without asking? The woman sounds out of control. Good for her. Like the rest of her body parts, her hair is her own and she's free to do whatever she wants to with it. Should she have consulted you first? This depends on your social contract. If the understanding is that she needs to ask your permission before doing something that's entirely her business, then she's in clear violation of, not just the letter, but the very spirit of repression. To this, Uncle Mike says, go girl. To you, Uncle Mike says, butt out. The woman is, supposedly, your friend. She's certainly not your possession. Knowing, as you do, what love really is, you must have discovered its first rule is that everyone gets to be who they are. Your friend is someone who changed her hair color without warning. Were this the biggest change you'll ever see in her, she'd need to be part of the plant kingdom. Uncle Mike senses the real issue here is control, or your perceived lack of it, and would encourage you to contemplate her navel instead of your own. Has it occurred to you she might have wanted to surprise you? That she thought you'd be pleased at her new image? Trust Uncle Mike, if the young woman gets more attention as a blonde, she's aware of it. There could be a message here. You, of course already know it. In closing, Uncle Mike agrees that you have a right to your feelings. You also have an obligation to examine them for signs of dry rot.

• • •

Dear Uncle Mike,

My daughter sends me your columns from Oregon and I often find them interesting, provoking and humorous. I have no personal problems but would like to know your feelings about astrology. She also sends me your horoscope column which I very much enjoy. I know little about the subject, but I had my chart interpreted several years ago and found it to be amazingly consistent with what I know of myself; which, being fifty-six, is a good deal. My husband, a wonderful man otherwise, says astrology is hocum. He's a retired engineer and will have nothing to do with 'pseudo-science'. How unscientific can astrology be if it successfully describes individual nature? That's my question to him and now, to you. Thank you for your time.

Evelyn P., St. Louis, Missouri

Dear Evelyn,

You're more than welcome. The first thing that must be said of astrology is that it works. As a system, it describes human nature as an alchemical process. There are positive signs and negative signs just as there is bipolarity in the physical world of emission and absorption. There are four elements (fire, air, water, and earth) just as there are four elementary quanta (proton, photon, electron, and neutron) and four forces of nature (the electromagnetic, the gravitational, the nuclear, and the weak interaction of decay). If, with this set of qualities and modes, the universe manages to create and recreate itself, Uncle Mike has no difficulty imagining the plots of the human comedy to be extensions of the same equations. By dividing the yearly circle of 360 degrees into twelve signs reflecting triune aspects (cardinal, fixed, and mutable, or initial, steady state, and transmissive) of the four elements (modes of energy), and charting the planets in particular positions on this circular grid, astrology becomes humanistic trigonometry. From the view of empirical science, what makes astrology indefensible is the problem of action at a distance: the planets are too distant to have an influence on human affairs. We know now that every bit of matter in the universe is linked to every other bit in a way not subject to spacetime; which is to say, simultaneously, independent of time and distance. Nothing in quantum physics makes astrology a pseudoscience. If nothing else, remind your husband of Isaac Newton's response when asked how a preeminent man of science could believe in astrology. "I have studied it, sir. You have not."

• • •

Dear Uncle Mike,

Hi. I am a sophomore at the Elko High School. I have never really read your section, until recently. It was brought to my attention by my English teacher, Mr. David Hayes. As an assignment he has had us write to you, Uncle Mike. I am writing to ask your advice on problems dealing with my parents. About a month ago I had a really bad attitude about a lot of things and I showed it. My Mom started grounding me at important times and my Father turned his attitude towards me worse than before. At first I was upset, I did not understand why all this was happening. I have been doing my best to change my attitude and stop with my bad language, I feel I have succeeded. The only problem is I am still being punished for things my parents requested me to do. My Mom and I barely talk. I tell her things about school or other things and she never cares to listen. My Father does not speak to me or even care to look at me. I'd like to know or hear what you have to say. Maybe you have an idea on why my Parents act like I do not exist. I'd also like to know why most parents look past the good things we, as teenagers, do and never seem to miss the bad?

Stacy C., Elko, Nevada

Dear Stacy,

Thank you for your letter. Although Uncle Mike has been a teacher, this is his first time as an assignment. He's a little nervous but will try to keep his essay shorter than Moby Dick. Uncle Mike is sorry things aren't going well for you just now. Don't doubt for a minute they'll change. Your mission, if you choose to accept it, is to make sure the change is for the better. From what you say, you're making all the right moves. Good for you for admitting to yourself and your parents that your recent behavior left much to be desired. This puts you miles ahead of many, if not most, adults. And good for you for following through and doing what needed to be done. Talk has always been cheap and it's gotten a whole lot cheaper since being a victim has become a status symbol. Uncle Mike doesn't know much, but he's pretty sure about this: life is either something that happens to us or something we make happen. Taking responsibility for your life isn't just more fun, it's less work in the long run. Ever noticed how tired you look when you feel life's being unfair? Or how little time you want to spend with someone who's whining? Fortunately for us all, the world's not as complicated as it seems. Always and forever, we get what we give. Give love, get love; give respect, get respect; give trust, get trust. It's the simple physical truth behind the greatest moral advice: treat others the way you want to be treated. It's not called the golden rule for nothing. It's called the golden rule because it's the only one we have to remember. If things at home are as you describe them, your parents are behaving badly. If Uncle Mike were their father, he'd send them to their room. Rather than moping about the injustice of it all, try to understand. Your mom and dad are afraid. They're afraid for you, that you're developing the sort of social skills that lead to unhappiness; and they're afraid for themselves, that they've failed as parents. Anger is a reaction to fears we don't understand. Your parents are humans who are, just like you, doing the best they can. Sometimes, like now, it's a pretty poor showing. Have the sort of faith in them you want them to have in you and work toward positive change. Be the best possible version of yourself, not just for them, but because it's your responsibility to a universe that spent billions of years coming up with who and what you are. If you and your folks aren't speaking at the moment, sit down and write them a note. Tell them what you're feeling. Apologize for your past actions and let them know you understand why they deserve an apology. Tell them you're determined to do better and ask them to do nothing more than watch. Tell them you love them and want them to be proud of you. Tell them for Uncle Mike that they jolly well should be. As for why adults notice what's wrong with teenagers more often than they notice what's right, try not to take it too personally. Trust Uncle Mike, they can be every bit as critical of the weather, let alone of their fellow adults. Because it's your duty as an apprentice human being to question the rules, you just make the easiest target for people with unresolved control issues. Think of it as a challenge.

• • •

Dear Uncle Mike,

Why won't guys take no for an answer? I'm a 23 year old college student and there's this guy in my accounting class who keeps asking me to have coffee after class. He's a nice guy and everything but I'm just not attracted to him and am running out of polite excuses. My friends think I should just tell him to get lost but I don't want to hurt his feelings. I don't even want to go to class anymore. What do you say to someone who's obviously clueless?

Pursued in Portland

Dear Pursued,

Uncle Mike would suggest the truth. You ask why 'guys' don't take no for an answer. They do, dear, all of their miserable, frustrated lives. This young man is putting his ego on the line by expressing his interest. If you have none, you should let him know as gently and as firmly as possible. Making excuses solves nothing because it leaves the poor mope room to dream his impossible dreams. Honor his feelings and make yours known. Anything less would be gutless, which some people would maintain is several steps down from clueless.

· · ·

Dear Uncle Mike,

My brother was caught smoking, he is thirteen years old. He had been addicted for a year. My father tried to break him of it. He made him smoke a pack of non-filtered cigarettes. Do you think this is a cruel punishment? Or is this an effective way of dealing with this? I would appreciate your advice. Sincerely,

Katrina Diana, Elko, Nevada

Dear Katrina,

Having abused tobacco for many years, Uncle Mike has little advice to give. Does he wish he'd never started smoking? Absolutely. Does he plan to quit? No. He figures it's only a matter of time before smokers are rounded up and put on a reservation. This is part of his retirement plan. Because he smokes, there's a good chance he won't live that long. So it goes. That's how addicts think. Uncle Mike is sad to hear your brother is smoking. Is being made to smoke a pack of unfiltered cigarettes a cruel punishment? No. Cruel punishment would be if your father didn't care. Is forced overdose an effective way to kick the habit? For some people. For others, it just gives them a taste for unfiltered smokes. The decision to quit is your brother's to make. But you can tell him for Uncle Mike he may be making one of the biggest mistakes of his life before he's old enough to know better.

Dear Uncle Mike,

An old girl friend is coming back to town to visit friends. Since I'm one of them, she asked if she could stay at my place for a few days. She's dividing her time between three of us so as not to burden anyone. This is fine with me. We were together a year but that was two years ago and we've managed to maintain our friendship. I'm looking forward to seeing her. My girlfriend is freaking out. I've explained until I'm blue in the face that there's nothing romantic between us and she'll be sleeping on the couch. She says she trusts me but it's still not okay. Do I insult an old friend or risk losing a new one?

D.K., Portland, Oregon

Dear D.,

Interesting word, 'friend'. You fail to mention your old friend's age but, if she's over twelve, she'll probably be able to understand how sleeping on your couch might bother the woman who (pardon Uncle Mike if he jumps to a wrong conclusion) at least occasionally sleeps in your bed. Women are funny about things like this; unlike men, who get deadly serious. You were a prize nitwit, and an insensitive lout, to have agreed to the arrangement before consulting the woman who has a right to suppose she's an important part of your life. Either call your friend, explain the situation, apologize, and ask if she can find another place to stay. Or, invite your new friend to spend those days with you. She might be thrilled at the chance to get down with your old girlfriend. Pardon Uncle Mike while he snorts up his sleeve. The gesture would, at least, give her an option you had neither the brains nor the class to give her before. Either way, bucko, you've got some fence mending to do. Also, some attempts at clear thinking. Uncle Mike won't insult you by suggesting the possibility that having an old lover sleep over for a few nights isn't the surest way to avoid temptation. He can tell from the firm handle you have on things that you're immune to weakness and poor judgment. Uncle Mike must snort again. Before you're an hour older, you should ask your girlfriend to forgive you. You've insulted her in ways you don't understand. Uncle Mike recommends you get busy understanding.

Dear Uncle Mike,

Here's one for you. I'm a 46 year old professional woman, married for 17 years. My work involves frequent trips to Seattle and a young man I know through business has made unmistakable gestures. I'm afraid I'm very tempted. I love my husband dearly but our lives are lived largely apart. We have a comfortable domestic life but romance is mostly a memory. I don't want to end our marriage, only enjoy the attentions of an attentive younger man. There is no danger of my becoming a schoolgirl and running away from home. There is no way my husband would find out, as he's not a suspicious man and I'm an intelligent woman. I'm running out of reasons not to have a liaison with this young man. I sense from your column you're a man of some experience. I have no friends I'd wish to burden with this issue and so would like your thoughts.

Call Me Rachel, Wilsonville, Oregon

Dear Rachel,

Uncle Mike thinks you're a bored woman who's about to be reminded of the difference between excitement and pleasure. It's good that you love your husband. Lord only knows what you'd do if you didn't. You say romance is mostly a memory. This is a complaint so common among couples whose relationship has lasted longer than their VCR that Uncle Mike suspects it might be part of the human condition. Fooling around is part of the human comedy. Uncle Mike is no one's idea of a puritan and is familiar with the statistics on extramarital affairs: not quite as epidemic as owning a pet, but close. He's heard many stories about how a well managed assignation can revive and save a marriage. He's also heard about trickle down economics and waging war for peace. The least that will happen is that your life will become riddled with small dishonesties and complications you'll only be able to share with the person who's at the heart of them. The most that will happen is that your little out of town gambol will drive a wider wedge between you and your husband, even if he's deaf and blind, and that your marriage will fall apart like a cheap pair of shoes. Uncle Mike strongly suggests you find a hobby that doesn't involve breaking promises, turning someone you love into a pitiful dupe, and blurring the distinction between romance and cheap melodrama.

• • •

Dear Uncle Mike,

Reading your article about Stacy C., why her parent's wouldn't talk to her anymore, really started my blood to boil. After all, what does she expect a medal for her actions to her parents? She as well as other children have no respect for their parents, not accepting rules of their home. If they would only realize their parents love them and want to give them advice best to make them a better person, but children think they are mean and don't love them.

Well, I have a few pointers to give them. First you have to have love and respect for your parents, as they are raising you, putting food on the table, clothes on your back, roof over your head. They don't ask you anything other than you to have a lot of love and respect for them as well as others. If the parents can't trust you for your word and actions, then you had better get your act together, because some day you will go out into the workplace and you will fail in every job you face, as with friends as well, with your attitude. When you go on your own, make your own living, I'm sure you will find your parents were the ones to get you there and you will look back to know that your parents did love you and wanted to trust you.

Uncle Mike, I want to know who changed the laws that give the children ideas that parents can't lay a hand on them if needed? Children know and I've heard them say, if you hit me I'll call the cops and have you arrested. I've read newspapers about children turning their parents in for correcting them when they needed it. Uncle Mike, now day's children are raising parents. The parents aren't able to raise their children as the law says different.

When we were raised, we didn't talk back to our elders because we knew we would be punished. We grew up to have love and respect for our parents and they loved us too. When we were told "No", they meant it. We knew not to ask again. But that isn't today's rules. My father always said, "As long as your feet are under our table, you will respect our rules." Yes, we all grew up, never one of us (7) with a "jail" record of any trouble and we have all informed our parents how proud we were of them, making us a

90

better person with a lot of love and respect for young and old.

Till the time comes you don't have your parents around then you will realize they weren't so bad after all.

I just had to write you as Stacy C. isn't alone but I hope she will sit down with her parents and talk things over and listen to them about her problems. I'm sure she will feel lots better if she loves her parents.

Thanks for listening, Uncle Mike. Just had to get this off my chest. Happy Holidays to you.

Sincerely,
Mrs. Marlene Anderson, Halleck, Nevada

Dear Mrs. Anderson,

Thank you for writing and amen to most of your thoughts. To them, Uncle Mike would only add that the world is a much different place than it was when you and Uncle Mike were growing up. Children learn through example and the example set by parents and society today leaves a great deal to be desired. Our children are being raised by television, the family has become a two wage earner consuming unit, and respect isn't a value, it's a demand. Bless your heart for caring enough about Stacy's problems to write. Uncle Mike hopes she reads it and recognizes the compassion behind your concern. Happy holidays to you and yours.

· · ·

Dear Uncle Mike,

A long time back, you quoted someone about men and women, something about if men told women they were something and women told men they were something everything would be better. I forgot what the somethings were. Could you fill in the blanks for me? My boyfriend and I could use some help.

'Amy' in Portland, Oregon

Dear 'Amy',

All of us could use some help filling in our blanks. The advice you're talking about came from, of all people, Norman Mailer, an author who writes life much better than court records indicate he lives it. Paraphrased, Mr. Mailer said this: Most of the problems between men and women would disappear if, every day, men told women they were beautiful and women told men they were brave.

For best results, Uncle Mike recommends reversing the messages every so often. To the howls of the politically correct, Uncle Mike can only say that it's possible to say something gender specific without being sexist. Good luck to you and your gentleman friend. This might be a good time to mention Reverend Billy's Three Rules for Living Together on the Planet: Everybody eats, nobody hits, and there is no third rule. Fortunately for us all, life's less complicated than it seems.

• • •

Dear Uncle Mike,

Why do boys act so stupid around girls?

Five Girls in Eugene, Oregon

Dear Girls,

The reasons vary depending upon which stupid boy you're talking about. Generally speaking, boys act stupid because they're nervous and want to impress you. They keep it up because girls often reward stupid behavior. With luck, most of you will get over it.

• • •

Dear Uncle Mike,

I'm writing you in hopes you might be of some help in dealing with pushy neighbors. My husband and I just bought our first house. It's a small house in what I guess you'd have to call a downscale neighborhood. We like it, it suits our needs, and we thought it was time to build some equity and then move up when we're able. The neighborhood's not blighted or anything but it's mostly populated with low or middle level working class people.

My husband and I are both professionals just starting our careers and knew before we bought that we wouldn't "fit in". But since we're both private people who keep to ourselves, we thought there would be no real problems. We were wrong. Our neighbors to one side are a couple our age. That's the only thing we have in common. He's a security guard and she assembles electronic parts.

They're nice enough but just aren't people we'd choose to socialize with. They, especially she, seem determined to make us their friends. Neither my husband nor I have the time or inclination to develop a relationship with these people. The problem is that they refuse to take no for an answer. In spite of the fact that we have turned down every invitation to "come over and have a beer", "come help us eat this barbecue chicken", or "come over and play some cards", they persist. We don't want to be rude but the situation is getting intolerable and we're running out of excuses.

Suggestions please?

Disillusioned Homesteaders, Portland, Oregon

Dear Homesteaders,

Uncle Mike suggests you invest every spare nickel in lottery tickets so you'll be able to buy the home and neighborhood you imagine you rightfully deserve. He questions your use of the word 'disillusioned' since, from evidence you offer, many of your illusions remain hilariously intact. By the axioms of the real estate market, you're living in the house and neighborhood painstakingly determined by your place in the fiscal pecking order. Young professionals or not, your net worth and take home pay render you working class. As brave new property owners, you either learn to live with this or start a revolution. Judging from your letter, Uncle Mike would suggest the former.

Although not your cup of tea, people would fall to their knees in thanks for neighbors whose worst traits involved inviting you to eat their food and drink their beer. As unacceptable as they are, your neighbors aren't parking their motorcycles on your front lawn, firing random rounds through your walls or, as in the neighborhood of your dreams, encouraging their wolfhound to make poo in your herb garden. To say your expectations of life are out of synch with the real world is to push the envelope of diplomacy.

This said, on to your neighbors. As someone once pointed out, most of the problems of the world would disappear if people just minded their own business. Part of minding your own business is the willingness to allow other people to mind theirs. If your neighbors have a fault, this is it and, short of moving or burning them out, you're stuck with it. If you turn down their invitations long enough, they'll give up and accept the fact you have no use for them. Given human nature, they'll then become even less attractive neighbors. Uncle Mike respects your right to limit your social engagements but would encourage you to take this opportunity to work on your woefully stunted social skills. It would kill you to drink a beer with these people? Your personal space is so fragile it would be shattered by eating badly presented barbecue? Your time is too limited to exercise what were once called good graces? If so, your real problems hardly involve your neighbors. If nothing else, next time you snub these people, remember they're the ones who, while you're out building your future, will be around to call 911 when somebody else's neighbors come for your entertainment center.

• • •

Dear Uncle Mike,

I am writing you for a school assignment and for myself. I have a problem. I am 15 years old (I will be 16 next month), and I am almost 4 months pregnant and haven't been to school very much. I know that I need to go to school, but I am ashamed of myself for being pregnant at such a young age. Not only am I pregnant but I am not with the father of the child. My question to you is what should I do?

Sincerely, Rebecca Marshall, Elko, Nevada

Dear Rebecca,

Although life can seem complicated, the answer to your question is always simple. You do what you feel is right. If you know you should be in school, you should go. You have nothing to be ashamed of. You did something you decided to do with no intention of hurting anyone. Your decision had important consequences. The universe is about to deliver new life through you. Honor both it and yourself. It may be hard to realize now, but there are no mistakes in life. It's no accident you're going to be a mother and being pregnant doesn't make you a bad person or a victim. Uncle Mike isn't going to tell you your new path is going to be easy. Just remember it's your path and, if you watch where you're going, it'll take you where you want to go. If you decide not to go to school, decide to ask your teachers for help in studying at home. Life is what we make of it. Make it a good one for you and your child.

• • •

Dear Uncle Mike,

Here's one for you. A friend and I are making up a list of the worst ideas of the twentieth century. To give you an idea: manifest destiny, communism, going off the gold standard, credit cards, trickle down economics, the war on drugs, tabloid television, and fast food. We thought you might have something to add or might ask your readers to send in their favorite bad ideas. Even if you don't, thanks for the column. It's sure more fun than Dear Abby.

                    Dos Amigos in Portland

Dear Dos,

Uncle Mike is glad you enjoy the column and thinks your project should be funded by the federal government. This would of course appear on their list of bad ideas. Uncle Mike would add to your list: the citizen as consumer, religious political action committees, subsidized oil production, the notion there's a place we can throw our garbage, the elevation of Donald Trump and Roseanne Barr to the level of role models.

• • •

Dear Uncle Mike,

Why is it that guys can play football, but not girls? We may not be able to play as good as them, but we are not totally useless. And we try just as hard as they do. I've been told that we can't play because we are girls and we're just supposed to stand there and look cute. Or we can play, but it's only for them to tackle us so they can get something. They won't let us play when we're messing around at lunch. Why is this? No I'm not sexist, but I would really like to know why girls can't play football. Thank you very much.

Sincerely, D.C., Elko, Nevada

Dear D.C.

First, the good news. As several female high school students around the country are demonstrating, girls can play football, or at least place kick. Uncle Mike thinks girls will be allowed to play all positions the minute they prove they can, and honestly want to function as an agent of brute force. There will be a women's professional football league the minute some corporation is convinced people will pay to watch female warriors break each other's bones and celebrate reaching goals by performing stupid happy dances and uttering sounds most often associated with nonhuman primates. Uncle Mike, sexist reactionary that he is, would die happily without seeing this. But your question has to do with fairness. The reason you can't play football is not, as you know, that you're supposed to stand around and look cute. The reason you can't play is that the boys don't want you to. Such as it is, American culture has few uses for boys who are outrun or tackled by girls. Boys aren't stupid enough to think this can't happen and would do anything to keep it from happening to them. Dumb, but there it is. Uncle Mike suggests that, rather than submit to being pawed in the pigpile, you and your friends start your own pick up game during lunch and invite any boy who wants to play.

• • •

• • •

Dear Uncle Mike,

Why is it that there is a stereotype against football players? When our high school team got our pictures this year it was pretty funny. The photographer thought we were the stupidest people in the world. He would say, "Put your helmet in your right hand. Just think of the hand you throw with." I was just wondering why everyone thinks football players are dumb.

Mike Mullin, Elko, Nevada

Dear Mike,

Stereotypes are always ugly, especially when they seem to fit. People think football players are intellectually challenged because the number of scholar athletes who play tackle is statistically insignificant. The valedictorian of Uncle Mike's high school class played tackle, the salutatorian was an end. The rest of the team crushed beer cans on their foreheads and dated cheerleaders with low expectations. If the impression people have of you and your teammates bothers you, Uncle Mike would suggest you band together to change it. There are no stupid people, just stupid actions.

• • •

Dear Uncle Mike,

My friends and I are worried about a friend of ours. She's twenty-four, really smart, really nice, and has a lot of friends. The problem is she's going out with a forty-six year old guy. We've all met him and he seems okay but I think any middle aged guy who dates a woman young enough to be his daughter has something wrong with him. We're all just sort of standing around waiting for our friend to wise up. We're worried that she's going to miss out on a lot by being with someone who doesn't fit in with her life. What do you say to someone you care about who you think is making a big mistake?

Eric S., Eugene, Oregon

Dear Eric,

In your case, Uncle Mike suggests you apologize to the young woman for thinking you know what's best for her. You say she's both smart and nice. You act as if she's stupid and neurotic. There's nothing intrinsically wrong with a woman in her twenties pairing with a man in his forties. It doesn't mean your friend is looking for a father figure or that her friend is a slavering pervert who can't cope with women his age. Young women are attracted to older men because of their experience and lack of testosterone poisoning. Older men are attracted to young women because of their spirit and their lack of emotional scar tissue. People are attracted to each other because being with each other makes them both feel good. It's unfortunate this process makes you feel bad.

• • •

Dear Uncle Mike,

I have a problem with my father. He doesn't seem to like any guy. Whenever I go out with my friends—guys and/or girls—he gets upset. A lot of my friends are even afraid to come over to my house! He says it's a good thing that guys are afraid to come over. I've shown him that I can take care of myself, but he doesn't trust my friends (the guys). I've had a boyfriend for almost seven months, and my father doesn't really trust or like him. My mother likes him and trusts him, but my father thinks my boyfriend is going to try to do something bad to me. Do you have any advice for me and my father?

Anonymous in Nevada

Dear Anonymous,

Uncle Mike has advice for everybody. That's why he's Uncle Mike. It's also why people often cross the street to avoid him. First, let's talk about why your father might feel the way he does. Young men (Uncle Mike refuses to use the term teenager) have a reputation that is, for the most part, richly deserved. Testosterone, the powerful hormone that drives much of their typically male behavior tends to short circuit most notions of sexual ethics. For many long years, male humans are driven to distraction by their

DNA's urge to replicate itself by whatever means necessary. The means necessary is, all too often, whatever female human is within reach. Having been a young male himself, your father isn't old enough to have forgotten the effects of testosterone poisoning. This only explains his feelings and in no way excuses his actions which, judging from your letter, are flirting with full blown neurosis.

You are a lucky young woman to have a boyfriend who respects your feelings. Please congratulate him for Uncle Mike. You should also thank your mother for having the good judgment not to confuse him for the young males she had to contend with when she was your age. Uncle Mike assumes she gets a word in now and then when she and your father are alone. You should tell her how much you appreciate her faith in both you and your friend. As for your father, there's probably precious little you can do, aside from doing nothing to reinforce his fears and hoping he'll take a long, hard look at the wedge he's driving between himself and his daughter. What people fear the most is the unknown. With luck, the more your father knows of your friends, and of you, the less overly protective he'll be. Have faith in his ability to change, work toward earning his trust, and believe things will eventually get better. Until they do, recognize that your father is behaving in ways he shouldn't because he loves you and doesn't want to see you hurt. As hard as it may be to see right now, he's doing the best he can dealing with a situation (raising a daughter) he's never dealt with before.

As for your father's suspicion of your friends, Uncle Mike must say he's never met them and has no way of knowing if his feelings are warranted or not. Being suspected of things you haven't done can make even adult humans behave in ways that reinforce the suspicions: being rude, disrespectful, uncommunicative, and irresponsible. Take a look at your friends and make sure this isn't going on. If it is, ask their help in giving your father a truer picture of who they are. The biggest mistake you could make would be to let his fears make you angry and resentful. You owe it to yourself to be a better person than that. Uncle Mike wishes you the best.

• • •

Dear Uncle Mike,

I'm writing to ask you a favor. My girlfriend thinks you're a saint. I tell her there's a big difference between the advice you give other people and what you do in your own life. Your advice is usually okay, nearly always, right on. But I'll bet you're as flawed as anybody else and could use some advice yourself sometimes. Tell your readers the truth and get my girlfriend to stop comparing me to somebody who exists only on paper.

D.R., Portland, Oregon

Dear D.R.,

Uncle Mike is happy to help. Unless the Vatican is keeping it from him, something they'd have no reason to do, Uncle Mike isn't on the short list. Or even the very long one. Uncle Mike doesn't think he's being treated unfairly. As he's said many times, he's just out here with his eyes and ears open and his mouth mostly shut, doing his level best to figure out what being a human means. He has his good days and his bad days. The good days are when there's a poker game, the bad ones are when there's not. In between, he bumbles along trying to do as little emotional damage as he can. Like yours, his life is a comedy of errors, some of them more funny than others, too many of them cause for embarrassment and regret. Please tell your girlfriend for Uncle Mike that there are legions of people who have, for one good reason or another, entirely given up on him. Fortunately, none of them are in his poker support group.

• • •

Dear Uncle Mike,

Do you think someone who's 26 and drinks two six-packs a day has a drinking problem? My girlfriend is on me all the time about it. I've got a good job, do almost all of my drinking at home at night, and I'm not violent or abusive. I just like to drink beer. I'm ready to look for a new girlfriend. What do you think?

B.C., Astoria, Oregon

Dear B.C.,

Uncle Mike thinks you're a moron. Not because you drink more beer than your liver and kidneys were designed for but because you're not bright enough to examine your habit. Being significantly more than seven in dog years, Uncle Mike knows many successful practicing alcoholics. Too many to cast stones through the walls of his glass house. We all have our weaknesses and our drugs of choice: alcohol, marijuana, sugar, money, gasoline, undeserved attention. Unless your addictions necessitate bopping someone over the head and stealing their wallet or bopping them over the head because it seemed like a good idea at the time, Uncle Mike is a firm believer in whatever gets you through the night. There are two danger signs with any indulgence: does it damage relationships you regard as important or does it interfere with your work? If you wish to continue your present habit, Uncle Mike suggests you cut your girlfriend loose. Should you choose to do this, you must promise yourself not to call her when you're drunk and lonely.

• • •

Dear Uncle Mike,

There is an issue about STDs. If you want the kids to learn about HIV, AIDS, and other STDs. My question is should the U.S. schools distribute or sell condoms in school?

Beaner, Elko, Nevada

Dear Beaner,

In a word, absolutely. When Uncle Mike was young and hormonal, the purchasing of condoms was a brutal rite of passage. If the squinty old codger behind the counter would sell them to you at all, he or she would do their level best to make you feel like pond scum. The success of this deterrent was registered in the significant number of adolescent females who dropped out of school to have babies they and their blockhead boyfriends were emotionally and economically unequipped to provide for. In those days, STDs had barely been invented: gonorrhea (which, for reasons still mysterious to Uncle Mike, was called the 'clap') and

101

syphilis. Your world is a much different and far more dangerous place and anything that makes it safer gets Uncle Mike's vote. HIV is a sexually transmitted plague that, contrary to the fall off in news reports, continues to rage like a wildfire. When genital herpes, genital warts, and chlamydia are added to the mix, anyone who denies young people easy access to prophylactics is, in Uncle Mike's opinion, committing a crime against humanity. And no, you should not be made to bring a note from your parents. Please remember that, all assurances aside, there may be no such thing as safe intercourse. There is safe sex, the safest of which doesn't involve another person.

• • •

Dear Uncle Mike,

My husband and I have been married for nine years. He recently confessed to having a year long affair with a woman he met through his work. I didn't have a clue. He says he ended it and I believe him but I am crushed and more angry than I've ever been in my life. We have no children and so the option of ending the marriage is there. I'm not really asking for advice since I'm not a kid and I know I'll make up my own mind. Do you think men know how much they hurt women by being unfaithful? Maybe if you said something, one of them would think twice. Thank you.

Disillusioned, Gresham, Oregon

Dear Disillusioned,

Uncle Mike is sad to hear you've been emotionally gutted by the man you love and hopes the jerk is so ashamed he has to shave in the dark. Do men know the damage they do by throwing honor, and their pants, to the wind? In Uncle Mike's experience, yes and no. With luck, they learn it in time. The lucky ones have good women to teach them. Uncle Mike once heard of a dynasty in China that demonstrated an advanced notion of justice. Those convicted by the court weren't allowed to leave until they understood the nature of their crime. Although this would constitute life imprisonment for many, it's a reflection of the way that life works. If your husband comes to understand what he's done, not just to you but to himself as well, he'll be free. If not, he'll be a prisoner

102

of his own lack of virtue. Your mission, if you choose to accept it, is to facilitate his search for the moral high ground. You can only do this if you've first found it yourself. The question you need to answer is, can you forgive this man? If not, you'll be nothing more than a deliverer of punishment and the only lessons he'll learn will be guilt and resentment. Think long and hard and behave in ways you'll be proud of later. If this means throwing his clothes from the upstairs window, be sure to tie them in knots first.

· · ·

Dear Uncle Mike,

Do you think that it is possible for a zebra to change its stripes? For instance, a fifteen year old sophomore that has been a basic screw up all of her life to suddenly change? I am that person. This year I have maintained a 3.16 average, haven't been in detention, and haven't skipped a single day of school. But even now more than ever my teachers and elders are treating me like I'm a criminal. Can you please help answer my question?

Niki Patton, Elko, Nevada

Dear Niki,

Uncle Mike would be pleased and proud to help answer your question, but it appears he's too late. You've answered it yourself with your actions. Although Uncle Mike has yet to see a former zebra, he's seen many former 'screw ups' who've reinvented themselves. Congratulations on being one of them. If your teachers and elders manage to do so well, he'll congratulate them too. In the meantime, remember this: you're only responsible for your own behavior. People are holding you responsible for who you were, not who you are. It's ugly and unfair, but life can be like that sometimes. You gave them reason not to believe in you and you're paying the price plus interest. On the bright side, it's more their problem than yours. Continue to be responsible, not just to change their minds, but to change your own. If it seems like the right thing to do, sit down with your teachers and tell them you're determined to turn things around. Any teacher worthy of the name will take notice and offer all the help they can. Good work is always rewarded. Have faith in yourself and in those who will, in time, learn to have faith in you.

• • •

Dear Uncle Mike,

If you're engaged and your boyfriend breaks up with you, are you supposed to give the ring back?

Carrie S., Portland, Oregon

Dear Carrie,

Although you left legitimate room for doubt, Uncle Mike will assume that your fiancé and your boyfriend are one and the same person. It scarcely matters. Legally, you are under no obligation to return the ring. This said, Uncle Mike is at a loss to understand why you'd want to keep it. The ring was given and accepted as symbol of a pledge. Your young man found reason, valid or not, to disavow his pledge. Whatever emotional value the ring has for you now probably isn't the sort of thing healthy people hold onto. Uncle Mike can't help but wonder on what occasions you'd think to wear it. If it's that important to you, the most appropriate way to display it would be stuffed and mounted on the wall. Give the bloody thing back. It's no longer yours.

• • •

Dear Uncle Mike,

I'd like to hear your take on the Asian economic crisis. Do you think we should bail these people out or just let them take the fall?

D.K., Aloha, Oregon

Dear D.K.,

As nearly as Uncle Mike can tell, the problem stems from banks daring corporations and governments to behave like drunken sailors on other people's money. This rarely works out in the long run. Should we bail them out? In Uncle Mike's opinion, no more than 'we' should have rescued the savings and loan business by parting it out and selling it off at pennies on the dollar to many of the same people who ran it into the ground. While the rest of the world works at McDonald's, the international banking community has been, in the last little while, taking in profits by the fork lift, much of it skimmed from the top of the Asian economic 'miracle' in which international corporations were licensed to cripple millions of working stiffs who can't afford a bowl of rice, let alone a Big Mac or a pair of hundred dollar sneakers. It's not called the human comedy for nothing. Since banks have traditionally had a problem with government intervention, Uncle Mike would think the possibility of global bankruptcy would offer them a wonderful opportunity to show their stuff. Let the international banking community bail its own idiot cousins out. And do it with family money this time. If it means the price of their stock goes down, let them eat ramen noodles and drive last year's Rolls Royce.

• • •

Dear Uncle Mike,

There are people at my school that are telling people I'm bisexual. Whether or not this is true is not the issue. My question is, what can be done about this?

Crystal J., Elko, Nevada

Dear Crystal,

Someone much wiser than Uncle Mike once noted that all wars result from people not minding their own business and/or wanting something that's not theirs. The people conducting a whisper campaign against you are two for two. The only thing that amazes Uncle Mike more than the fascination some people have in the affairs of other people is the amount of time they're willing to spend talking about them. Some parts of the human comedy are less funny than others. People gossip to achieve power, for themselves and over the subject of their slander. On a good day, Uncle Mike can drum up much compassion for anyone so riddled with doubts about their own worth that slicing and dicing someone else's reputation seems like their best shot. Your situation could be much worse: it could be you doing the whispering. What can be done? Always and forever, the only appropriate action is to live the truth; the truth here being that your sexuality is your business. Since real success comes from character, Uncle Mike recommends you seize the moral high ground. Don't react in ways that are beneath you and don't let your detractors see you sweat. While confronting weasels isn't Uncle Mike's style he might, if backed into a corner, look them in the eye and ask with genuine concern if anything in their own life had gotten the least bit interesting yet.

• • •

Dear Uncle Mike,

I had an unpleasant experience recently at my favorite restaurant. I had company from out of town and took them to dinner. The restaurant is quite close to my home so we decided to walk. I put $100 cash in my pocket. Bottom line: our check came to $102. I asked the waiter quietly if I could bring the balance and the tip in the next day. He brought the manager to the table, who promptly and not quietly told me, rudely, that they did not do business that way! My guests paid the remainder plus tip. I argued that we shouldn't tip. I also will not go back again. How would you have dealt with it?

D.D., Portland, Oregon

Dear D.,

Uncle Mike would have gone to a bank machine or walked back home for his checkbook. Regarding the tip, it's a gratuity based on the quality of service and has nothing to do with the management's shocking unwillingness to wait until tomorrow for payment for food you've eaten today. If the manager was rude, by all means don't go back. He has much to learn regarding business. So do you. In the best of all possible worlds, you could learn together.

• • •

Dear Uncle Mike,

I am thinking of writing a personal ad and would like to know if you think they are safe.

Lonely in Wilsonville, Oregon

Dear Lonely,

There's nothing the least bit risky about placing a personal ad. The risky part comes when you meet the people who answer it. Uncle Mike has heard many heartwarming stories of unrequited humans finding each other in the back pages of a newspaper.

Granted, all but one were in ads promoting the service, but Uncle Mike refuses to believe anything is impossible. The challenge with personal ads is the natural urge all of us have to make a good impression, and the unnatural urge many of us have to stretch the truth past all recognition. You'd never do this, of course, but the people who respond to your ad copy just might. In clinical terms, what you're doing is posting public notice of an open position and soliciting resumes (a French word meaning 'shameless embellishment'). What you'll find during the interview is that there's a darn good reason most of these people are unattached; something which could, in all fairness, be said of most of us.

Does Uncle Mike regard this as dangerous? Not if you have a good sense of humor. If it's your karma to date an ax murderer, the personal ads will only be the means of your meeting, not the cause.

The worst that will probably happen is you'll know even more people whose company you'd cross the street to avoid. Uncle Mike wishes you the best of luck and would love not to know how things work out.

• • •

Dear Uncle Mike,

After moving to Oregon from Iowa, relatives are asking if I've seen a Sasquatch. Despite several near glimpses among the denizens of downtown Portland, I cannot say that I've actually seen the big-footed bugger. How about you? Have you ever seen a Big-Foot? Ever attend a Sasquatch Potlatch?
Ned, the Iowa Boy

Dear Ned,

No, Uncle Mike has never seen a Sasquatch. But then, he's never seen Iowa either. He saw Kansas once, but it's been so long ago it might not be as frightening as he remembers. Uncle Mike is intrigued by your near sightings in downtown Portland and, as soon as you and your therapist sort out the details, he'd love not to know them. Should your luck change (for better or worse, depending upon the circumstances), Uncle Mike would recommend you not greet him or her with a hearty Midwest "Hey, you big footed bugger." Sasquatches are fairly laid back but, treated with disrespect, their behavior is probably every bit as abominable as any snowman in Tibet. Which explains why Uncle Mike has never attended a potlatch thrown in their honor. But then, being easily horrified, he also avoids karaoke bars.

• • •

Dear Uncle Mike,

Heard you were a Blazer fan. How about these guys? I think this team is headed for greatness. What do you think?

A. Fellow Fan, Portland

Dear A.,

Uncle Mike has no idea who you've been talking to but sincerely recommends you sever your contacts.

• • •

Dear Uncle Mike,

Why do football players always slap each other's butts? If cheerleaders did that they would probably get some weird looks from the fans. What do you think?

Anonymous, Elko, Nevada

Dear Anonymous,

Before beginning, Uncle Mike wants you to know he's completely out of his depth. He doesn't know any football players and, if he did, he can't imagine knowing one well enough to ask why he slaps his teammates' butts. What does Uncle Mike think? That slapping butts is better than slamming elbows into foreheads; which, given the spirit of the game, would be much less weird. It would never occur to Uncle Mike to slap anyone's butt in front of anyone whose butt it wasn't, but he has nothing against those who do. Unless, of course, they're cheerleaders. Cheerleaders should only giggle, hold hands, and bounce up and down. Unless they're male, in which case they can head butt each other.

• • •

Dear Uncle Mike,

I am a sophomore at Elko High School, in Elko Nevada. Our assignment is to write and ask you a question. My question is, what makes people gay? I have wondered this for a long time, and don't understand how someone can like the same sex.

Gina Micheli., Elko, Nevada

Dear Gina,

As nearly as Uncle Mike can understand, what makes people gay is the same thing that makes people straight, only different. The longer Uncle Mike observes his fellow humans, the more certain he is that sexuality is a spectrum rather than a polarity. Technicolor as opposed to black and white. Uncle Mike would encourage you to keep wondering about the roots of physical attraction. Regardless what our sexual orientations might be, the more we understand about sexual behavior, the less different anyone else's seems.

• • •

Dear Uncle Mike,

Frustrated is the only word I can think to use. My wife and I are currently building a new home. Though we have planned everything carefully and chose our contractors with care, it seems they never show up as scheduled. Their other projects are running longer than they planned, etc., etc. The work they were to perform is holding up subsequent work and now those subsequent contractors' schedules are filled on the new dates. I'm sorry I am rambling and am probably only blowing off steam but maybe you could give me a few good phrases that could be used on the delaying muffs that won't get me sued or thrown in jail.

Frustrated in Port Angeles, Washington

Dear Frustrated,

Uncle Mike forgives you for rambling and thinks it's nothing but okay that you're blowing off steam. Uncle Mike used to share your frustration for things not going as scheduled. He feels much better since he realized that everything happens at just the right moment and the real problem was his nitwit attempt to predict a future filled with variables over which he had little or no control. He still makes plans but no longer confuses the road map with the actual trip and tries to control nothing but his own actions. As for what you might say to these irresponsible swine, it depends upon how fast you want your house built. If you're not above pouring the foundation yourself, when the little primadonnas show up with the trucks, tell them today isn't good for you and you'll get back to them when your schedule clears. At which point they'll either sue you or react in ways that will allow you to have them thrown in jail and you and your husband can get on with assembling your yurt.

• • •

Dear Uncle Mike,

I have a problem that maybe you could help me with. My best friend has been great to me ever since I moved here. She has been there in times of need and in times of laughter. But lately she has been really rude to me, she always cuts me down, tells me how to act and what to do. I didn't really notice this until one of my friends told me what she has noticed, and now that's all I notice. I've tried dropping hints and sticking up for myself more, but she doesn't get it. I don't want to tell her straight up because she will get mad and probably won't want to be my friend anymore, and I cherish our friendship, and don't want to lose it. I have talked to my parents and they always say that I should tell her and if she gets mad she isn't worth worrying over, but she is. I have wondered what it would be like if we weren't friends and I don't think I could stand not having her as my friend. It has gotten to the point where I have told my parents that I want to move so I don't have to worry about it anymore, and they have tried. I don't want to write her a letter because one of my other friends did that and she got really mad and started talking about her behind her back to everyone including me. I don't want that to happen to me and I don't want to lose her friendship. She has been great to me when I needed her most but I don't understand what's gotten into her lately. Is there some advice you can give me about what to do that I haven't already gotten?

Concerned in Nevada

Dear Concerned,

It sounds like you're already up to your ears in advice. Your problem stems from not taking any of it. There's nothing wrong with that as long as you're willing to go on eating abuse for the sake of friendship. There's nothing wrong with enduring abuse, unless it makes you sick, which it seems to be doing. Something needs to change. Your loyalty to this person is admirable and only you know how much loyalty she deserves. That's the first issue you need to resolve. It sounds to Uncle Mike like your friend is in a lot of pain. People hurt others because they've been hurt themselves. Silly, but there it is. Even sillier is the fact that they, and we, hurt the people who are closest to us and deserve it the least.

Not all of the human comedy is funny. What you need to do is find the source of her pain. Something has gutted her self-image, and her response, the least productive of any she might have picked, is to cut you down to size. Imagine how much she must be hurting to do this. Her life is a mess and she may be jealous because yours isn't. When people try to control other people's lives, it's because they feel they can't control their own. She may be pushing you away to fulfill a feeling that no one in their right mind would have anything to do with her. She may be testing your friendship, something she needs to learn not to do. What you can be sure of is that she's feeling frightened and alone. As a friend, it's your mission to show her this isn't true. Without making a big deal of it, take any opportunity you have to tell her what you love about her, what it is you admire and respect. When she speaks cruelly, tell her how happy you are you're her friend and not her enemy. "This is just your way of saying you love me, right?" There is, of course, the distinct possibility she no longer values your friendship. Things happen, people change, life goes on. Be the best friend you can be, not just to her, but to yourself. Every relationship is different and each has its own rules of engagement. You may need to change the level of this one. Your parents aren't as wrong as you imagine. Honesty is the hardest part of love. Delivered with care, it's the greatest gift we can give to each other. Let your friend know her actions are hurting you. If worse comes to worst and you lose an acquaintance who was once a friend, trust Uncle Mike, you'll survive the loss. As someone once pointed out, there are times when the best thing you can do is just get on your horse and ride away.

• • •

Dear Uncle Mike,

My husband's son is 14 and lives with his mother. He comes over most weekends. The two of us have never gotten along, a real personality clash, but we're civil and all. Last weekend, ten dollars was missing from my purse. No one else was in our home but him. I haven't told my husband because he's got a temper and would be real mad. I just wish he'd not come over but that won't happen of course. I'm (upset) because I can't leave my purse just lying around. How do you get a kid to stop stealing?

Drafted Mom, Astoria, Oregon

Dear Lady,

If you don't mind Uncle Mike saying so, you're a real piece of work. The youngster in question is your husband's son. If his welfare is not your concern, you should desert your post and retire to a cave where you can further hone your talent for ignoring the needs of others. Children steal because they feel powerless and imagine that money, or hubcaps, will provide it. The only power that deserves the name is love. Surprising as it might seem, the young man probably thinks you don't care about him, that you might even wish he weren't a part of your life. Like it or not, you're part of his, and your role as an adult (there's a chuckle) is to give him the tools he needs to have a life instead of a case history. If 1) you're certain the ten dollars was there and that your husband didn't take it, and 2) you think the boy's father would behave badly if you told him your suspicions, keep your dealings between you and the young person you're role modeling for. Next weekend, hand him a ten dollar bill. Tell him a boy his age needs some spending money and you forgot to give it to him last week. No, this isn't rewarding bad behavior, it's encouraging a healthy sense of shame, and letting him know there are people he can trust. The real trick is being one.

• • •

Dear Uncle Mike,

My girlfriends are always complaining that their husbands and boyfriends are slobs and they have to follow them around picking up their dirty clothes. I should have it so good. My boyfriend is a neat freak. We're both 26. Before we moved in together, I thought it was funny and cute, the way he sorted his shirts by color, never let there be more than five dirty things in the sink <u>counting silverware</u>, and was always there with a coaster. We've been living together for two months now and I'm fighting the urge to kill. I'm not a slob but the sight of a sweater on the back of a chair doesn't bother me and doing last night's dishes

113

before I make dinner doesn't ruin my evening. I love the guy and have really tried to clean up my act but there's no compromise and no way to measure up. We used to have great sex. Now, when he lights a candle and puts on some music, I half expect him to start dusting and arranging pillows. Is this something that works itself out in time?

Melissa, Beaverton, Oregon

Dear Melissa,

Everything works out in time, this being what time is for, but experience shows that some situations work out better than others. Yours is one that often doesn't. Young people should be taught by their parents and teachers that the first rule in selecting a mate is to make sure your standards of cleanliness and order closely coincide. Should you and your partner decide to stay together, you must both accept that living in hell together is better than being apart. Many successful marriages are based on this principle. Throw from your mind any thoughts of changing him and suggest he do the same with you. Ask him not to arrange your sock and underwear drawer, regardless how much of a jungle it might be. Do your share of the house drudgery on your own schedule and don't be prodded into obsessions not your own. This will, of course, drive him crazy. The ability to love you anyway is a trait that will either develop or not. Uncle Mike waves to you from the dock and wishes you fair sailing. As for the sex part, when you picture him dusting, imagine him in harem pants.

• • •

Dear Uncle Mike,

I'm writing you to get some advice. I am currently a high school student looking for a part time job. I was hoping to find something just for a couple hours after school. My only dilemma is that my mom disagrees with me. She thinks that I shouldn't have a job because she doesn't want my grades to drop. I promised her that I would keep my grades up while working, but it isn't working. What can I do to convince her to let me work during the school year?

Anonymous in Elko, Nevada

Dear Anonymous,

To be honest, probably nothing. Your mother is acting in what she thinks are your best interests. She could, of course, be wrong. Your job is to wonder if she might be right. The first thing one should always ask about money is how much it costs to get it. A part time job is more than a couple of hours after school. It's a set of new relationships and responsibilities, a rechanneling of energies, and a shift in focus. Having seen the effects of these things in her own life and the lives of others, your mother is concerned that your studies will suffer. She knows you much better than Uncle Mike and Uncle Mike would stuff a sock in his mouth before second guessing her. Aside from keeping your grades up and pointing out friends who are successful at managing good grades while working, the only thing you can do is wait for your mother to change her mind. Or you might walk your talk by devoting a couple of hours a few days a week to doing domestic chores as if your mother were paying you minimum wage. You might both learn something from the experience. Especially if you put your tips into a college fund.

• • •

Dear Uncle Mike,

How different do you think men and women really are?

Joe S., Seattle

Dear Joe,

As different as they can be without one rendering the other extinct. Rather than being a problem, this is what makes the dance such fun. It took thousands of millions of years for life to discover sexual reproduction. If it was an accident, it has proven a persistent one. Sexual identity is a spectrum but sexual distinction is polar and complementary. One needn't be a Nobel laureate in biochemistry to figure out the ability to bear a child, to say nothing of the experience of actually doing it, fundamentally sets one apart from those designed to impregnate. Plainly put, estrogen is not testosterone, and it never will be. Women and men live in

115

conceptual universes they can explore but never accurately map. Sexual union is a celebration of difference, love is the way the universe ensures we'll never stop engaging the mystery. Women also shop more.

. . .

Dear Uncle Mike,

About three and a half years ago my grandma was diagnosed with lung cancer. The doctors operated on her and took one of her lungs. She goes regularly for checkups and two months ago they found cancer in her other lung. The doctors have done everything possible for her and they give her one year to live. My grandma stays with us so we can take care of her. It's hard seeing her like this, but there's not much a sixteen year old girl can do. How can I cope, or help her? Any advice?

Anonymous

Dear Anonymous,

Uncle Mike's advice to you is the same advice he gives to himself: love and cherish what you have for as long as you have it. The great lesson that death teaches all of us is that we take our lives and the people in them too much for granted. Rather than the first day of the rest of his life, Uncle Mike greets each morning with the realization this could be his last one on the planet. It helps him prioritize things. People die every day and few of them ever see it coming. Like all living things, your grandmother's days are numbered. Knowing roughly what the number is can, and should, give you both a new lease on life. The sadness is not that your grandmother is going to die. All of us do that. The sadness would lie in not appreciating her while she's alive. Spend as much time with her as you can and ask questions about her life. Who was she as a girl? What is she most proud of? What's the best advice anyone ever gave her? How did she and your grandfather meet? What was your mother like as a child? What we all realize as we get older is that there's much more to people than we thought. Learn from this woman so that who she is will live on through you.

You can also use this time to learn what you can about death

116

and decide for yourself what it is and how you feel about it. Uncle Mike stopped believing in death years ago when he learned there was no room for it in the equations of quantum physics, our best picture of the way things are. Behind the world of form, the universe exists as consciousness. Each point of it is self aware. You, your grandmother, and Uncle Mike are all point conscious observers: unique, one of a kind perspectives of the unfolding of creation. Like every other perspective, we were all there at the big bang and will be there for the next half of forever. Everything is in motion, busily on its way somewhere else. Uncle Mike's body is busily on its way to system breakdown and recycling. His consciousness sees this as a change in perspective rather than a tragedy.

· · ·

Dear Uncle Mike,

I'm 28 and my girlfriend is 24. We moved in together four months ago. A month ago her 17 year old sister moved in with us. She wasn't getting along at home so we told her she could stay with us and finish out her senior year. She started flirting with me the day she moved in. My girlfriend mostly laughs it off. I did too at first but it's getting worse. Nights when she's at work, her little sister walks around in a towel or watches TV in a long t-shirt and no underwear. This isn't my imagination. She goes out of her way to rub against me and when we're alone her good night hugs aren't innocent. She knows I know she's coming on to me but pretends she's just kidding around. This is driving me crazy. It doesn't help that my girlfriend and I aren't getting along great right now. Short of moving out, I don't know what to do. One of these nights I'm going to weaken. She keeps reminding me she'll be eighteen in two months.

B.L., Portland, Oregon

Dear B.L.,

Uncle Mike suggests you remind yourself you could spend little sister's birthday behind bars. Depending upon your part of her good night hugs, you might already be in violation of some very serious laws. The moral situation is even worse. You know better, she apparently doesn't. What you're dealing with is a kitten sharpening her sexual claws on her big sister's boyfriend. Entire soap opera subplots are built around scenarios like this and, unless you'd like to see your social network dissolve along with your opinion of yourself, you don't want to act out your converging urges.

Although a trusting person by nature, Uncle Mike has a hard time believing that, if your girlfriend knew what was going on, she'd be laughing it off. By tradition, older sisters can read younger sisters like cheap novels, which can only mean that most of the low rent dalliance you're dallying with takes place behind your partner's back. This behavior makes you a swine. Since you're the card carrying adult, and have chosen to keep you and Lolita's business to yourself, it's your responsibility to apply the bucket of cold water. Gently but firmly tell the little temptress to put some clothes on, knock off the flirting and get started on her homework. Tap your own forehead with a mallet and direct your attention at the woman you're supposed to be involved with. With all due respect, you don't sound like a pillar of strength. If neither relationship gets better quick, Uncle Mike suggests you do the manly thing and run like the wind.

• • •

Dear Uncle Mike,

Maybe you can help with this problem. I would like to have a comfortable relationship with someone, but he makes it difficult. He continually makes Fervent Promises, but consistently delivers Faint Performances. He's a good guy, but his flakiness hurts. Any suggestions?

Burned

Dear Burned,

Uncle Mike sees three options: lower your own standards, persuade him to raise his, or kick the dust from your boots and ride away. Not knowing either of you, Uncle Mike has no idea what he's promising and why, how fervent his promises are, and how faint his performances might be. Being a man more than seven in dog years, he has more than a faint inkling. What you're asking him to promise are behaviors for which, after nearly a million years of social evolution, male humans have displayed absolutely no knack. They form a veritable constellation of behaviors whose visible spectrum runs from monogamy and emotional availability to taking out the garbage and giving back rubs without being asked. Without question, men would be much better persons if they were able to learn, or even admit their stupidity and wrongness, but after twenty-five years of intense consciousness raising (all dates being either before or after Ms. Magazine), the success rate remains discouraging. As Tammie Wynette put it so well, "after all, he's just a man."

Which scarcely means you shouldn't continue to bear down on him if the spirit moves you. Be the gentle ox goad that herds him to perfection. Devise a system of rewards and punishments that molds his nature more closely into what you have in mind. Women have incredible power over men, which explains the fear and suspicion men feel when they bond with them. In terms best suited to a bumper sticker, testosterone hates to lose. Whether by habit or biochemistry, men suspect that in order to be who women need them to be, they must cease to be who they are. This is, in large part, true. It's also true if you swap genders. Men fear what you fear: the loss of self. Part of what makes mating and bonding so funny is that what preserves a sense of self in one person, close emotional bonding and interdependence, decays it in the other. There being no accidents in the universe, Uncle Mike suspects we're all supposed to learn something from this. What physicists know so far is that the equation of the cosmic marriage between Emission and Absorption (the roots of the tree of good and evil) is different and equal. You describe your friend as a "good guy". This speaks well for his ability to, given time, grasp the fundamentals of having a relationship. Only you know whether the pearl is worth the price.

• • •

Dear Uncle Mike,

What do you think of prejudiced people? Who cares of other people's religion, culture or color? What's the main reason for people hating other people?

Maria U., Elko, Nevada

Dear Maria,

People hate what they fear and fear what they don't understand. Many of them live alone and frightened in a world so small that anything, or anyone, different is a threat. Racial and ethnic hatred is usually learned, and so, can be unlearned. Our country's population is changing from a predominantly white Anglo-Saxon culture into a multi-ethnic one. Hopefully, being thrown together more often will help us all understand how much more alike than different we are. As for what Uncle Mike thinks of prejudiced people: that he hopes they feel better soon.

• • •

Dear Uncle Mike,

Just curious. As a liberal, can't-we-all-just-get-along hypocrite, what do you think of Slick Willy now? I'd love to hear you defend the slime ball. Consensual or not, Monica Lewinsky is a kid.

No Fan, Portland, Oregon

Dear No,

Uncle Mike is glad you took time from your obviously un-pleasant life to scribble a few insults and half-baked opinions and send them off to him. You need all the release you can get and writing letters sure beats sitting on the porch shooting rats. To clear your confusion, Uncle Mike is not now, nor has he ever been, anyone's idea of a liberal. As a lad, he was a conservative; which is to say, very good at behaving and playing the game. As a young man, he was a radical; which is to say, an active and disruptive agent for change. Those were the days. These days, Uncle Mike is a conservative radical who votes for any party endorsing the equations of quantum physics and the lyrics of Bob Dylan. This may make him a progressive.

But you were squealing and snorting about Miss Lewinsky. Uncle Mike must question your use of the term 'kid'. She is, both legally and functionally, a young woman. Like you, and here all similarities must end, Uncle Mike knows about her only what he reads in the newspapers or is force fed by cable. While filled with compassion for anyone forced to attend Beverly Hills High, Uncle Mike cannot bring himself to cast Miss Lewinsky as a young waif in a riding hood. Only in a time when everyone is a victim would anyone think to call her one. Like the rest of us, she's responsible for her actions and, even if they involve the President of the only superpower on the planet, you can't imagine how little they interest Uncle Mike. Neither are they any of his business.

What does Uncle Mike think of President Clinton now? That he's done some good things for the country, sold out some things he shouldn't have, is doing the best he can, and evidently has a hard time with monogamy. The first three are matters of public concern, the last is between Mr. Clinton and his wife.

• • •

Dear Uncle Mike,
Is it ever proper for a woman to open a door for a man? Whenever I do it, I get strange looks.
Cynthia S., Portland

Dear Cynthia,
Like many others before you, you've confused Uncle Mike with Miss Manners, Ann Landers or her dear sister Abby. Unlike them, Uncle Mike is studiously ignorant of etiquette: the Byzantine set of rules and rituals devised by the idle classes to make the rest of humanity feel socially challenged. Uncle Mike regards it as no accident that the word comes to us from the French,

a culture that calls pancakes 'crepe', or that its literal meaning is 'ticket', as in: we have one and you don't. Etiquette-wise, even in the self-righteously egalitarian nineties, it's probably a social gaffe for you to open a door for any male not obviously infirm or disabled. It's also uncouth to use your salad fork to decorously twirl your spaghetti into the spoon you mustn't use for the soup. But then, it's hard to imagine why anyone in their right mind would care. If the spirit moves you to open the door for someone, Uncle Mike sees no reason the configuration of their reproductive hardware should enter into your decision. Of course, Uncle Mike thrives on strange looks and takes pleasure in performing those acts of consideration his mother taught him were the basis of good manners.

• • •

Dear Uncle Mike,

One of my friends is really getting on my nerves. I want to tell her off but I don't want to be rude to her. What should I do?
Anonymous, Elko, Nevada

Dear Anonymous,

As the first step in resolving any problem involving another human, Uncle Mike recommends self examination. Is there something you're doing that could be unsettling to your friend? Is her behavior the only thing that's getting on your nerves? Are you being overly sensitive or judgmental about something that's not a large deal? Are you just reacting negatively to change, a favorite reaction even among those old enough to know better? If the answers are all no, you have three options: accept your friend's behavior, do something to change it, or redefine your relationship. Changing the behavior of others is a tricky business and, if what you're shooting for is positive change, you're right in assuming that telling the young woman off isn't the best approach. Uncle Mike has yet to witness a situation made better by being rude. Deal with your friend the way you'd want her to deal with you should your behavior ever run its fingernails down the blackboard of her life. People behave badly for one of two reasons: they're either afraid or they need attention. Try to understand why she's being unpleasant. Although coming right out and asking her isn't cheating, you'll learn more by trying to figure it out yourself. It's also a good reason to ask your parents or other elders what they think and to think about what they say. Remember what you like most about your friend and why you value your relationship. Tell her. Then let her know in subtle ways (by laughingly shoving your fingers down your throat or tapping her forehead with an imaginary mallet) when her actions are pushing you over the edge. If she cares, she's a friend. If she doesn't, she's an acquaintance. Much depends on learning to distinguish the two.

· · ·

Dear Uncle Mike,

I've been reading your column for several years now and, although I don't always agree with your advice, I very much enjoy your mind. I especially like your thoughts on quantum physics, a subject I know nothing about but am now at least interested in, and about consciousness not being subject to death. These are strange subjects to find in an advice column. You needn't answer me in print but I would be interested to know what sort of God, if any, you believe is consistent with what you know about the universe? Or do you make it a practice not to speak of such things?

Call Me Lucy, Portland, Oregon

Dear Lucy,

The only things Uncle Mike makes it a practice not to speak of are the private affairs of people who are not in the same room. Uncle Mike believes in a universe that is, beneath the bells and whistles of observed reality, a unified field: all things are one thing. What we observe is a thin membrane of object events on an undifferentiated and unmanifest sea of probabilities. The organizing principle that transforms what might be into what is, is consciousness. Every object event in the universe, ourselves included, is a point conscious perspective of infinite potential. This limitless possibility is the unity that rests behind the illusion of difference, like a final Burma Shave sign saying nothing: all that is, added to all that was, multiplied by all that might be. The God of quantum reality doesn't play dice. The God of quantum reality plays poker.

• • •

Dear Uncle Mike,

My husband and I recently asked my sister's daughter to babysit for us. This is nothing new, she is fifteen and has watched our two sons age five and seven many times. She is a level headed girl, the boys like her and it gives her some extra spending money.

We have always trusted her but this time we came home early and found her lying on the couch with her boyfriend. They were both fully clothed but 'Carmen's' blouse was rumpled and partially unbuttoned. It was obvious there was some heavy necking going on. I was shocked she would do this, my husband got very angry and threw the boy out almost bodily. 'Carmen' swears nothing happened and I'm inclined to believe her but I feel she still violated our trust. She apologized of course and said she'd never do it again and begged me not to tell her mother. I told her I would have to think about that. I know my sister would be furious and would punish 'Carmen' harshly. I'm really torn because 'Carmen' is a good kid, but my sister is my sister and she should probably know what's going on. My husband thinks so. What would you do in a situation like this? I don't know now if I should have her babysit anymore.

Worried Aunt, Eugene, Oregon

Dear Worried,

Unless the harsh punishment 'Carmen' would receive involves vicious beatings and the use of shackles, her mother should be made aware of her experiments in biochemistry. Assuming your niece is normal, her promise she'll never do it again applies, at best, to not doing it on your couch when there's the slightest chance you'll walk in. Like water finding its own level, the newly hormonal always find a way. Unless your sister is a hopeless neurotic whose reaction will do more damage than good to Carmen's budding sexuality, she needs to know how far the budding has progressed. If your relationship to your niece is a close one, you should use this opportunity to counsel her on the minefield she's tap dancing through. You should also tell her you expect her friend to apologize, in person, to you and your husband for having violated the rules of your home. At some point, your husband should put his hand on the lad's shoulder, look him straight in the eye, explain the role of uncles in relationship to young pups sniffing around their niece, and ask how much of a man he imagines himself to be. It won't stop him but it might slow him down and will almost certainly keep his sneakers off your couch. As for whether Carmen should be allowed to watch your children: in Uncle Mike's experience, people who are trusted are more likely to be trustworthy than those who aren't.

. . .

Dear Uncle Mike,

How are you supposed to tell someone you like them, without embarrassment?

Anthony F., Elko, Nevada

Dear Anthony,

Uncle Mike is reminded of a story. A young man stops an old passerby on the sidewalks of New York and asks, "Could you tell me how to get to Carnegie Hall?" The old man looks at him and says, "Practice." So it is with all of the hard parts of life. Embarrassment is the price we pay for making stupid mistakes and, to Uncle Mike's way of thinking, there's nothing stupid about telling another human you like them. Since people generally respond well to compliments, a good way to start is by telling the person something you like about them. Bear in mind the world is full of cheap talk and that actions speak louder than words. If you treat someone with friendliness and respect, they'll know how you feel, just as you're able to tell if someone likes you or not by the way they look at you. Life's not as complicated as it seems. If you speak your heart, what comes to you is truly yours. This includes rejection and the feeling you're as insignificant as pond scum. With practice, this feeling almost goes away.

. . .

Dear Uncle Mike,

I have a rather delicate problem. A dear friend of mine has been going through a hard time (a bad relationship finally ended) and has gained a considerable amount of weight. She is a very pretty woman whose features are not enhanced by the extra pounds. Nor are her chances of meeting another man which, because she is lonely, is an important issue. Aside from a few veiled, joking references to my own waistline in hopes of bringing about a discussion, I have said nothing. Have you any suggestions?

A Friend, Portland, Oregon

Dear Person,

Aside from encouraging you to mind your own business, Uncle Mike has no help to offer. Your friend knows far better than you how much she weighs and, even if she didn't, it would not be your place to tell her. Friendships have ended and wars have begun with the mistaken notion that the world is waiting breathlessly for us to tell it how to be better. You say your friend is lonely. Good for her. Like poverty, loneliness is a great teacher. You say she needs a man. A more important issue is whether or not she wants one. Uncle Mike doesn't believe in accidents and has noticed in his own life that what comes to him in the way of people and events is, for better or worse, what's his. Hopefully, your friend understands this better than you and will use her solitude to examine the reasons for it. People with the blues (a term Uncle Mike finds more useful than 'depression') sometimes fill the emotional void with truffles and ice cream. This is called getting through the night, a process that won't be hurried along by 'friends' telling them they're porking out. Uncle Mike would encourage the both of you to look on the bright side. At least she's not become critical and meddlesome.

• • •

Dear Uncle Mike,

I have a problem. I'd been working at the car wash for about a month and a half when a new girl got hired. She sucks up to the manager and bosses everyone around even though she doesn't have the right to. She took my job which gets more pay than the rest of the jobs. What should I do?

Austin S., Elko, Nevada

Dear Austin,

You posed your question well. There are many things you could do. What you should do is watch carefully as her karma unfolds. Uncle Mike assumes your take on the situation is accurate, that you're not confusing 'sucking up' with being a harder and more enthusiastic worker, or 'bossiness' with accepting responsibility for the efficiency of the workplace. The only work you need to concern yourself with is your own. Sooner or later, we all get the rewards we deserve and if the young woman is dealing from the bottom of the deck, she'll find the extra money will be more expensive than she thought. Just go on reminding her politely that she's not your boss, let alone your superior. Remind yourself that people who can be sucked up to are people who got where they are by sucking up. Your real work is to be sure you don't become one of them. If the situation deteriorates beyond anyone's ability to bear, you and your fellow workers might consider strapping the little corporate climber onto the top of minivan and running her through the wax cycle. Good luck on your next job.

• • •

Dear Uncle Mike,

I'd be interested to know your thoughts on physician assisted suicide. Would you ever consider it, and if so under what conditions?

Just Catherine, Seattle

Dear Just,

Uncle Mike has difficulty imagining the reasoning involved in deciding this is a legal question. To what sort of mind, Uncle Mike asks, would it occur that what Uncle Mike does with his body is anyone's business but his own? Uncle Mike suspects that future historians will laugh and laugh. No civilization worthy of the name regards the bodies of its citizens, as the property of the state and, regardless of one's personal feelings about drinking hemlock, supporting the notion that our lives do not belong to us is a crime against humanity. Would Uncle Mike consider taking his own life? This is, of course, none of your business but, since you were gauche enough to ask, Uncle Mike is polite enough to answer. First off, you must remember that Uncle Mike doesn't believe in death. Uncle Mike, a devout quantum relativist, sees no room for it in the equations and no evidence of it in the observable world. Systems dissipate, bodies deteriorate, and energy reconfigures itself. Through it all, the point conscious perspective that is Uncle Mike goes on, a dimensionless drop of awareness which existed as potential before the big bang and will spend the next half of eternity experiencing the dance of infinite possibility. At play in the fields, that sort of thing. Would Uncle Mike consider recycling the mortal coil he's had so much fun with? Only if he were convinced he was trading up. While Uncle Mike doesn't believe in death, he has a healthy respect for and a strong dislike of a) intractable pain, and b) being unable to wipe drool from his chin. One of the nice things about getting older is knowing when it's time to go home, a process Uncle Mike thinks of as reshuffling the deck.

• • •

Dear Uncle Mike,

Whenever I get a copy of Upper Left Edge (Cannon Beach, Oregon), I read your column because it's so entertaining...usually. I do think you missed the mark when you answered "Drafted Mom". While your style might be purposefully caustic at times, you were too hard on her—and possibly too soft on her stepson, depending on his motives. He may need attention, but many kids (like my "behavioral" students) are very good at tweaking adults in order to get something. Here is what I would offer her.

—It's normal to feel angry at a child who does something wrong. Some stepkids are difficult to like because they do try to sabotage the new family. You don't have to have warm fuzzy feelings towards a child to act fairly. Your actions count more than feelings here. Be fair without faking affection.

—Find a support group for stepfamilies. You'll learn that you're not alone, and you might also learn some valuable hints.

—Your first responsibility is toward your spouse, and toward your children if you have any. Angry teenagers sometimes try to disrupt family life, so you and your husband must present a united front. Have a family conference, but let Dad do any disciplining. Most counselors agree that the biological parent should handle discipline matters during the first years of remarriage.

—If you must choose between being liked and being respected, choose respect. Respect may not come till later, but it's worth it.

—He may choose to not like you. Kids have more power of choice than adults give them credit for. Try to get to know him. If he doesn't accept your offers of friendship, let it go. Continue to act fairly.

—Let him know that while his behavior may be understandable, that doesn't make his actions acceptable. This will help him learn accountability—a useful skill!

—Don't try to be his mom. He already has one.

—Just do your best. Grownups are human too. Blow off steam with your girlfriends (I did this a lot when my stepson lived with us!). Don't assume full responsibility for making the family work

—Dad and son need to put in some effort too.

—Eventually kids grow up and get a different perspective. Hang in there!

Been There and Done That
Vancouver, Washington

Dear Been There and All That,

Uncle Mike is tickled pink you find his column entertaining, usually. He feels much the same about the letters he receives. Although he stands foursquare behind his "purposely caustic" response to Drafted Mom, whose husband's son she suspected of stealing money from her, he's happy for the chance to pass your advice along. Perhaps, to return the favor, you could pass along a mild warning from Uncle Mike to the young humans you refer to as "my 'behavioral' students." Beware of adults who describe you with personal pronouns.

• • •

Dear Uncle Mike,

I would like your advice on something. I like this guy and he likes me. But my parents won't let me date him. When I say something about me and him doing something they freak. I don't know what to do. The don't have a good reason for it either. They won't because he's in a different religion. But he treats me real well. And I don't know what to do.

Anonymous, Elko, Nevada

Dear Anonymous,

Uncle Mike recommends you follow your parents' wishes. Not necessarily because they're right, but because they're your parents. At the same time, do everything you can to change their feelings about your friend. If possible, put them together with him in a group. Let them see who he is. Talk about your problem with another adult in the family, listen to their opinion, and hope they'll intercede with your parents on your behalf. As a last ditch effort, your friend could call and ask your folks if they'd allow him to visit and plead his case. Even if they don't change their minds, they'll respect him for it. No matter what, honor their decision.

Although any Absolute worth believing in couldn't possibly be amused, people still kill each other over religion; forgetting that, although there is only one mountain, there are many paths. Count this as your first lesson in why stereotyping and prejudice aren't behaviors you want to buy into. Uncle Mike wishes you and your friend the patience and calm persistence it takes to change the world.

· · ·

Dear Uncle Mike,

Have you a ready solution to the problem of barking dogs? Our new neighbors have a high strung German shepherd who should be getting hoarse by now but isn't. He barks night and day, often without reason, always when we so much as step out of our house. We rarely see the owners and, aside from greeting them coolly, haven't made our feelings known. Suggestions please?

Silent Sufferer, Portland, Oregon

Dear Silent,

There's much to be said for suffering the costs of civilization in silence but, from the sound of things, you've gained all you can from the situation. The problem is not, of course, the dog. The problem is the humans who have, or in this case have not, properly raised and cared for it. The dog is barking because its humans have made it nuts by confining it to a small space and imbuing it with an exaggerated sense of threat. In a perfect world, it would be them who would be licensed and shipped to the pound if they became a nuisance. The social contract demands diplomacy. Make a point to encounter your next door idiots and tell them the constant barking is a violation of the spirit of neighborliness. If it continues, which Uncle Mike is willing to bet large amounts of money it will, ask if there's anything special the animal control people need to know about their situation before slapping them with a fine. The last alternative, one Uncle Mike would likely follow, is to suffer a bit longer in hopes that the dog will eventually triumph over its neurosis. Barking may be a drag but euthanasia is forever.

· · ·

Dear Uncle Mike,

What do you think about a husband who reads his wife's personal e-mail and then gets jealous over what he's read?

Heidi in San Francisco

131

Dear Heidi,

Much the same as he feels about being asked questions that lack the parameters necessary for an intelligent response. For the sake of polite discourse, Uncle Mike will assume the offending message made no mention of a recent episode of wild abandon, or confirm plans for a future excursion into the dark heart of infidelity, or otherwise contain passages purple enough for a jury of adults to see as grounds for a male hissy fit. Given these conditions, your husband's wounded ego hasn't a leg to jump up and down on. You may remind him for Uncle Mike that, in the days when messages from a distance came in envelopes, he would be guilty of both mail tampering and violating the privacy of a human who, in the best of all possible worlds, would be his most trusted and respected friend. If, as Uncle Mike assumes, the message was addressed to you alone, his decision to read it was a serious violation of social contract. A person puts up with this sort of behavior only at great risk to the long term quality of their life. Uncle Mike has a shameless love for simple truths. Conflict begins when we mistake someone else's affairs for our own. Wars begin when someone takes something that isn't theirs. Assure your husband such behavior is beneath him and that much depends on his ability to resist it.

• • •

Dear Uncle Mike,

I know it's rude to ask another person's age but my friend and I would love for you to settle our bet. You have evaded the question in the past, saying only that you are roughly "seven in dog years". We take this to equal 49. Our wager involves which side of 49. I don't expect you to answer this in print and would actually prefer you didn't since it would probably only be another coy veiling of the facts. I have included a stamped, self addressed envelope for your response. We enjoy your column immensely by the way and, were we not old enough to know better, would make some effort to lure you out to dinner.

"Thelma and Louise", Portland, Oregon

Dear Ladies,

You have made Uncle Mike happy as a puppy. First, by being old enough to know who would, and would not, make a good dinner companion. And second, by giving Uncle Mike a stamped envelope. He already has a bottle of whiteout and is very committed to recycling. Pushing onward, Uncle Mike must question, along with everyone in his poker support group, your choice of the word 'coy'. This does not constitute a denial, of course, but only raises a question. Uncle Mike would love to tell you how old he is, if only because it would mean the universe is a place where absolute answers can be found. Time, as Einstein pointed out, is (aside from being a mental construct superimposed upon observed change) relative, depending upon the velocity of the observer in terms of his or her reference frame. You can see how this complicates things. The faster an observer goes, the slower time passes, a phenomenon we all know to mean that the spacetime metric is about as absolute as a water balloon. This makes the age of any observer (or, as Uncle Mike prefers to think himself and others, point conscious perspectives) is the sum (and product) of a long (perhaps endless) string of relative increments of relative time states. It's lovely, but quite the mess. Although Uncle Mike is able to reconstruct some of these states in his mind, his memory isn't what it used to be and he's certain he's left some things out. This hopelessly mars any attempt he might make to set down the equation for his age. Just when he thinks he's got it, a new question arises about his actual velocity on some night in question. (Time goes fastest when you're sitting, or lying, still.) Yes, Uncle Mike could walk over to the calendar and come up with some horribly rounded off figure that laughs in the face of the actual time line of his life (a time line of point consciousness that, like every other, began with the big bang and will go on unraveling for the next half of forever), but he has far too much respect for the truth (and Heisenberg's Uncertainty Principle) to play fast and loose with quantum reality. As nearly as Uncle Mike can figure, his real age, like yours, lies somewhere (and simultaneously) between younger than springtime and old enough to know better. If you send Uncle Mike another stamped envelope, he'll investigate the notion of 'birthday'.

. . .

Dear Uncle Mike,

What do you think about legalizing marijuana? I feel that they should in hospitals but nothing more than that.

Miranda, Elko, Nevada

Dear Miranda,

Uncle Mike thinks all drugs should be legal, their sale licensed, and their revenue taxed. Not because he thinks it's okay for everyone to use them but because he thinks the time and energy necessary to catch and imprison those who do could be better spent making a world people didn't have to get drunk or stoned to forget.

. . .

Dear Uncle Mike,

Six months ago, I found out my wife was having an affair with someone at her office. We've been married for nine years and finding out just about killed me. I've almost left several times. Our sex life is almost nothing, every time we start, I imagine her with this jerk, who I've never met, and I'm either unwilling or unable to perform. She feels bad and guilty and says it won't happen again, that she was lonely and needing some excitement and romance in her life. She's really trying to make it up to me and I know she loves me and that I love her. But after this long, I don't know if I'm ever going to be able to trust her again. A buddy of mine who thinks I should stick it out says I should have an affair of my own so I can see how that it doesn't mean I can't still love my wife and that I can't learn from it and not do it again. I don't know what to do so I'm not doing anything hoping something will change. If there's any advice you could give me to get through this or over it, I'd be grateful.

Don't Use My Name, Salem, Oregon

Dear Don't,

Uncle Mike doubts you can get over anything without going through it. Going around doesn't even work. The art of being human requires much on the job training and the lessons you're learning at the hands of your wife are worth every bit of what you're paying for them. The first thing Uncle Mike recommends is that you find the largest cork you can and jam it into your buddy's mouth. Advice is cheap; unless it's bad, in which case it costs an arm and a leg. The idea right now is to find your center, not abandon it by using another human being to test your feelings about the importance of fidelity. Your wife has, bless her cheating little heart, given you a splendid opportunity to find out what you're made of. Both legally and morally, she's given you grounds for divorce. The fact that, after six interminable months, you've chosen not to a) throw her out on her keester, or b) leave yourself, means you're either a) a hopeless mope who's begging to be walked on again, or b) a promising student of the human condition. Only you know if this woman can be trusted or if she's worth the trouble it will take to find out. Only you know if the husband you've been to her is the man she wants and needs. Only she knows how sorry she is she played you for a chump. Only you know if you can forgive her. If you can't, there's no point in the two of you wasting any more of each other's time. While you're making up your mind, remember the woman you thought she was and treat her the way you'd want her to treat you if you'd emotionally gutted your marriage and were feeling lower than worm droppings. Be, in short, the best human you can be. Good humans who are willing to be good friends make the best husbands and wives in the world.

• • •

Dear Uncle Mike,

I have a question about Saturn's rings. How is it possible for our sun to make flowing debris, such as the rocks that make up Saturn's rings, to take on different colors like blue, yellow, and red? I have always wondered how light could travel so far, have a large proportion of it absorbed then be divided into the light spectrum and then come all the way back to earth.

Leigh M., Elko, Nevada

Dear Leigh,

Uncle Mike is happy to hear you have no personal problems great enough to outweigh your curiosity about the rings of Saturn and the nature of light. The colors we observe, whether in the rings of Saturn or the eyes of our sweet babboo, are the colors not present in the object itself. The colors that are there are absorbed, the colors we see are reflected. Trees are every color but green, fire engines aren't red, and Leonard DeCaprio's eyes are every shade they're not in the movies.

• • •

Dear Uncle Mike,

Well, I hope you like giving advice on the sinister topic of love. I am currently living with my fiancé' (I guess you could call him that; I have yet to see a ring). I am 21 and he is 12 years older than I, divorced with two kids. We have been together a year now. In the beginning of our relationship, he was always expressing his feelings to me. I remember feeling like he was almost "too" much, he ALWAYS wanted to be near me. About six months ago, I really fell in love with him. And now, the tables have turned. He has come from a terrible divorce and I have come from several bad relationships myself. We have a terrible communication problem. Last night he walked away from a conversation in which we were both frustrated. Which left me to spend a night alone for the first time in a long time. He gets very defensive when I tell him that something he did hurts me. How do I talk to him in a way that he will listen? How do I react to this?

Heartbroken and Questioning, Portland, Oregon

Dear Heartbroken Questioner,

Fortunately for all concerned, Uncle Mike enjoys giving counsel on all matters not pertaining to which fork to use. You ask about love. Unless there are some strengths and delights to your relationship that you failed to mention, it sounds like half of your engagement is disengaging. The dance you describe is called approachavoidance, much like the tango only more ancient. Regardless how egalitarian a pair bond turns out to be, it begins with a pursuit: a constellation of primal, often brutal behaviors which, performed artfully, constitutes courtship. During the six months before you fell in love, your suitor was, in Shakespearian terms, wooing you. Putting its best paw forward as it were. Your avoidance invoked his approach. At the moment you opened yourself, flower like, to his professed devotion, the dynamics of your little tango changed. Once a person gets past the hysterical weeping, one of the funniest things about love is that the person who cares the least has the most power. You have become, in business terms, a done deal.

Uncle Mike isn't suggesting for a minute that this is the best you can, and jolly well should, expect in the way of male behavior. If, for instance, what your fiancé' was really interested in was sharing a life with you, your acceptance of his suit would exalt his soul, precipitate a you've-made-me-the-happiest-man-in-the-world experience, and make him vow to live up to the honor you've paid him. Such a person would pour more energy into the system, not less. Giving the swine the benefit of the doubt, this may be a   reflex that will pass in time. Real relationships with women tend to terrify men; who, living as they do in an entirely different biochemical universe, have a need for emotional aloofness wise women eventually cease trying to understand. Although gender distinct behaviors are, for the most part, myth, male humans resist being absorbed with a strength only matched by the female humans who, with the purest and best of intentions and no small amount of patience, devote their lives to absorbing them. On a good day, it's all quite amusing. Given time, your male may learn to face his phobias like a man and recognize you as a faerie sent by his karma to remind him of a purpose higher than himself. From what you say, Uncle Mike wouldn't bet on it.

In dealing with his fellow humans, Uncle Mike finds what works the best is to see things as they are. This person's behavior is hurting you. The distance between you is increasing rather than decreasing. It's becoming more, not less, difficult to communicate. You seem to express yourself well, which leads Uncle Mike to suspect the reason your fiancé' is neither listening nor hearing is that he doesn't find what you're talking about all that interesting. What one does now is draw a line in the sand. Calmly and compassionately tell him that the person he's become isn't someone you'd consider spending the rest of your life with. Tell him that, your love for him aside, he has a decision to make and that, if he'd like, you'll be glad to give him a day or two to make it. As some philosopher must have said: life is short, a bum marriage is long.

• • •

Dear Uncle Mike,

This might be outside the scope of your column but I'd be interested to know your ideas on tax reform. Graduated tax, flat tax, or sales tax?

Amy in Eugene, Oregon

Dear Amy,

Uncle Mike thinks they're all just dandy. The graduated tax, expecting those who have more to pay more, seems like wonderfully good sense. Unless, of course, you have more and you want to keep it. Tax shelters were invented to prove, once and for all, that rain falls only on the poor who, bless their stalwart little hearts, are used to suffering. The poor, unable to see the large picture while wet and shivering, console themselves with the lottery. And, when that fails, bad drugs. Many, if not all, revenue enhancement goals would be would be met by the simple expedient of asking corporations to behave like responsible adults. A flat tax on all citizens, corporate and private, would, at least theoretically, level the playing field. The operant word is 'theoretically'. Being of sound mind, Uncle Mike doesn't plan to hold his breath until the people who play expense account golf band together on behalf of their caddies. As for the sales tax, Uncle Mike has long been a fan of user fees. A tax on consumption benefits those who consume the least, an idea whose time had best come soon. Uncle Mike strongly endorses levying a penny a roll tax on toilet paper and using the revenue to incinerate recreational vehicles.

• • •

Dear Uncle Mike,

I have a friend named Jennifer. She likes this guy named Rueben a lot, and sometimes she does things with him. One of her good friends named Jamie is trying to get hooked up with him, even though she knows Jennifer likes him. She tried to talk to her friend about it but she just won't get it through her head, and she is still trying to get hooked up with him. What should my friend do?

Carly in Elko, Nevada

Dear Carly,

The first thing your friend should do is learn the difference between friends and acquaintances. Friends are people who, when push comes to shove, will neither push nor shove you. They certainly don't purposely sink their talons into your gut. What should your friend do? Uncle Mike would suggest she accept a situation that isn't likely to change and encourage her not to compete. The object of the competition is a human being who will, in the end, decide for himself. As with any situation, your friend's best course of action is to be the best version of herself she can manage without putting on an act. If who she is isn't what the young man wants, the young man isn't someone she needs. Should he choose the predatory young woman who's stalking him, it will be because he has something to learn and she's just the teacher he needs.

• • •

Dear Uncle Mike,

I need your help. My girlfriend and I recently managed to move to a place in the country. We both love animals and have had pets all of our lives and our family now includes a dog, two cats, a cockatiel, and a recently acquired mating pair of rabbits. My girlfriend wants to add a pig. Although she'd mentioned it before, I didn't take her seriously. She's not talking about one of the small, pot bellied ones, but a real pig. She says they're no trouble at all, are smarter than dogs, and make great house pets. Do you know anything about this?

Mark in Portland, Oregon

Dear Mark,

Although Uncle Mike knows more about trouble than he does about pigs, he refuses to turn his back on you in your time of real need. That your girlfriend is giving the idea of living with a pig so much as a moment's thought says two things about her. First, that she's more lonely than anyone deserves to be and second, that she is one of the many victims of Walt Disney. Real pigs do not stutter irresistibly. They do not even oink. Real pigs snort and drool and, when they chase wascally wabbits, it's with an eye to eating them. It's often said that a pig, left to its own devices, is a clean and intelligent companion. Uncle Mike suggests you never leave your pig to its own devices. Little Porkey's cousins are wild boar. Ferocious, razor-tusked rodents who hunt in packs and regard food like you tame sport. Just because your domesticated, beady-eyed carnivore eats corn on the cob and apple slices doesn't mean it's never noticed the meat on your ribs or looked at your dog in ways your dog will wish it didn't. Pigs are, relatively speaking, smart as whips: leagues ahead of horses (although some would ask what isn't) and brighter than most dogs. Under controlled laboratory conditions, pigs have mastered the skills required to play simple video games. While this may qualify them, in theory at least, for work in the fast food industry, it hardly assures they'll be pleasant dinner companions. As for cleanliness, a pig who bathes regularly and never goes outside is much tidier than the average chimpanzee. Not only does this fall short of a glowing recommendation, strong evidence suggests that a clean pig is not necessarily a happy one. Like its near kin, the hippopotamus, your pig was born to wallow. Unless you're willing to thwart your pet's pursuit of personal bliss, you'll need to convert a portion of your back yard into a stinking mud pit. Properly cared for, your pig will quickly turn into a 200 pound hog, at which point the fun will be over.

· · ·

Dear Uncle Mike,

My husband and I just celebrated 35 years of marriage and I thought your readers might be interested in the story of how we met. We were both students at the University of Oregon and...

Partners for Life, Seattle, Washington

Dear Lady,

While Uncle Mike hates to interrupt someone hell bent on boring him into coma, he must. Your confusion stems from two unfortunate assumptions. First, that Uncle Mike is Dear Abby or her wholesome twin Ann Landers. The only similarity between Uncle Mike, Aunt Abby, and Auntie Ann is that they are all air breathers and pay the rent by making marks on a computer screen. Your second faulty assumption is that anyone outside the captive circle of your friends and family would find your story heart warming, elevating, or even interesting. No, not even the role played by your Pekinese. Uncle Mike is happy that you and your husband are happy together and appreciates, in ways you can't imagine, your willingness to share with him.

· · ·

Dear Uncle Mike,

The shroud of Turin is supposed to be the body length linen cloth that was laid on the naked body of Jesus after he was taken to the tomb. Some Christians believe that this cloth contains the blood and sweat outline of Jesus's body. If this is true then this cloth contains the DNA of Jesus. It might soon be possible to take Jesus's DNA and clone an identical Jesus. If we cloned Jesus there would be a fantastic religious revival in the world. However, the revival would be more effective if we cloned more than one Jesus. So my proposal would be to clone one Jesus for each church that was willing to pay the cost of their clone. It would also be fitting to have each church that wanted a clone to choose a young virgin girl named Mary so that each church could spread the good-news that their church had a virgin birth of a baby named Jesus. Maybe each church would also want a manger for the baby Jesus.

Name Withheld To Prevent Retaliation

Dear Gentle Believer,

Uncle Mike genuinely admires your spirit. This does not prevent him from worrying about you. The scenario you propose is a real dandy, the perfect way to celebrate the turn of a millennium by bringing on the apocalypse much of humanity is itching for. There would indeed be a "fantastic religious revival in the world", one that Uncle Mike would thoroughly enjoy watching from the safety of CNN. Uncle Mike can't help but think that a cloned Jesus, his advent heralded by Dolly the Sheep, would be any more amused by the world than he was before. And, once the spiritual fur started flying in the halls of televangelism, large mobs of unamused, well meaning Christians, blessed and spurred on by a religious bureaucracy that has, after much spiritual struggle, elevated money changing to tax exempt theme parks, would come for him with pitchforks and attorneys. He would, in modern terms, once again disappoint his sponsors. It would probably be the Bob Dylan tour that triggered things.

On the way to Golgotha, whose twenty-first century cloning would involve a "lone assassin", there'd be enough material for several Kurt Vonnegut novels. The Larry King roundtable with Pat Roberts and the Pope. The Barbara Walters interview on the mount. The Oprah sermon. The eternal Geraldo investigation. The last lunch at McDonalds. The last temptation by Bill Gates. F. Lee Bailey's pro bono insanity defense. Uncle Mike questions whether any civilization worthy of the name should put a simple carpenter through this twice. Can you imagine how depressing it would be if, two thousand years ago, you'd delivered a teaching of compassion and love based on the unity of all beings in the world behind this one. You'd managed, through the clarity of your vision, to illuminate the coded software of the life well lived in terms so simple children understood. You had, as a human being, walked your talk to the point of dying a slow death in order to show that the spirit in us and around us doesn't die. You'd hoped, probably even believed, that the truth would set the world free. And now, a large grant from an anonymous rich person to an offshore genetic laboratory has brought you back. In essence, to relieve the nagging boredom and maybe turn a buck or two. The temptation would be great to just shake your head, tell the world you'd already said everything you had to say, and wish the whole blind and ungrateful bunch of us happy trails. A better plan would be to take snippings from the shroud of Elvis.

. . .

Dear Uncle Mike,

I love to play soccer, but I hate most of my teammates. I don't think my coach likes me either. It makes me so confused I feel like I hate it now. Should I quit to get away from the people that annoy me or sweat it out and keep doing the sport I love?

Confused Athlete, Elko, Nevada

Dear Confused,

When Uncle Mike was a youth, he was taught that a winner never quits and a quitter never wins. It took him much of his life to learn this is utter nonsense. Uncle Mike doesn't play soccer, let alone love it. Uncle Mike loves to arrange words on paper. But if he found himself word arranging for a boss who didn't like him, with fellow word arrangers he thought weren't worth the powder it would take to blow them to smithereens, he'd find another gig. Unless, of course, he realized the problem was his. Watch your coach. See which players he or she likes and why. Unless they're kissing up shamelessly, emulate their behavior. Play your best game and, if your teammates don't respond with respect, shame them into better behavior by relentlessly complimenting their efforts. The only advice Uncle Mike can give you is to accept what is. If the place you're in doesn't feel right, chances are you're in the wrong place.

. . .

Dear Uncle Mike,

A good friend and I got into an argument last week and we both said some awful things to each other. Now when we see each other where we work, we go the other way. I think she feels as bad as I do but neither of us has apologized. I really miss her. But I wonder if I apologized if she would? Is this just being dumb?

Heather, Portland, Oregon

Dear Heather,

Yes, dear, you're being dumb. The first thing to do is to tell your friend the truth: you're sorry and you miss her company. Whether or not she apologizes is beside the point since the only behavior you're responsible for is your own. If she's a friend, and whatever it was you said wasn't something that would prevent her from a) ever trusting you again, or b) caring if you were run over by a truck, she's waiting for an opportunity to do the same. The second thing you should do is stand in front of a mirror, look yourself in the eye and say you're really sorry. Then wink, pat yourself on the shoulder and answer, "That's okay, Bozo. Just don't do it again."

• • •

Dear Uncle Mike,

I get down sometimes and have trouble getting back up. It's not like I need Prozac. I just need to be able to see out of the hole faster. Do you ever get down? What do you do?

Constant Reader, Newport, Oregon

Dear Constant Reader,

Yes, like most thoughtful people, Uncle Mike sometimes feels less than himself. For whatever reason, it seems to become shallower and more fleeting with age. Uncle Mike's great teacher on the subject was a gardener he worked with for a time planting bamboo in a Siberian tiger exhibit. One morning we were shoveling elephant manure in the rain and Mike was discussing his mother who was having a hard time. He suggested she stay busy. "It's hard to be down when you're doing something." Even shoveling elephant manure in the rain. Simply put, depression is inertia, the psychological equivalent of mass. In finer terms, depression is lack of motion. The world becomes a bitter fudge you're swimming through. This state, whose cause may be imaginary but whose effect is as real as a stone wall, was one of the reasons the Chinese invented firecrackers. It breaks the spell. What makes depression so little fun is that it's a biochemical state. One's neural circuitry is flooded and damped by what good science calls 'blue meanies'. Blue meanies may listen to reason but they're slow to respond. Thoughts are electromagnetic events, moods are their steady state background of chemical balances. Changing a mood involves washing psychoactive chemicals from your window on the world. It involves physical action: an increase or decrease in momentum. One either does something or, in the case of those experiencing mania, one stops doing it. How much of a surprise can it be that, when you're feeling down, you feel better when you get up? Take a voyage into the dark heart of your angst and discover the source of your fear and sadness. Ask yourself how little any of it will matter in a thousand years. Think positive thoughts, even when the feelings they induce don't last. Just as surely as the universe made little green apples, keep trying and they will. As more than one happy person has pointed out, it never hurts to look on the bright side. Find something to smile about, someone to smile at. Go to the park and watch dogs and children play. Meditate on just how blind and stupid it is to pull down the shades on a surprise party thrown in your honor by the forces of creation. Write a short essay on self-pity explaining the advantages of wallowing in worst case scenarios and pretending you're powerless. If all else fails, sit down and seriously count your   blessings, an ancient spiritual exercise only chuckled at by those who've not tried it. Uncle Mike who, in his time, has self induced some dandy dark states, has never got past three without feeling the sun peek through the dreck. It helps if he then remembers to make barnyard sounds. He generally begins with the cow, follows with the sheep, and closes with the duck. As my old gardener friend would agree, it's hard to take things seriously when you're quacking.

• • •

Dear Uncle Mike,
    Do you think Monica Lewinsky had a 'relationship' with President Clinton?

Angela, Portland, Oregon

Dear Angela,

Like you, Uncle Mike would have no way of knowing. Unlike you, the special prosecutor, and a news media behaving as if it were on bad drugs, he doesn't concern himself with the personal affairs of people he doesn't know.

• • •

Dear Uncle Mike,

What is your opinion on gambling? I think it causes problems with the family because my mom told me that her friend spent their whole savings. It's an addiction that's hard to stop. I'm concerned on your answer.

Dean O., Elko, Nevada

Dear Dean,

The gambler's addiction is to action and risk. Add the flashing lights and beeps of a video poker machine, and you've got a dangerous drug. Life is a gamble, filled with action and risk and Uncle Mike has no problem with those who thrive on it. Unless it gets in the way of their lives. Taking food and security from those you love is not the path of right action. More dangerous than the addiction of the gambler is the addiction of the dealer: in these times, federal and state governments who twitch at the thought of giving up their cut of the profits. There's a big difference between allowing citizens to gamble and advertising the lottery on television, and no society thinking clearly would encourage drunks to match wits with a video poker machine.

• • •

Dear Uncle Mike,

Before I begin, let me say I enjoy your column very much. Your wit and wisdom has brightened many a day for me. Why are you not syndicated more widely? Is there no justice in the world?

My question concerns the recent discovery that 45% of Americans are overweight. I read somewhere that the Romans got fatter just before their empire fell. I'd love to hear your thoughts on what the fattening of America means. Will overweight women become the beauty norm? Will male paunches become a power symbol?

Slim in Portland, Oregon

Dear Slim,

Before Uncle Mike begins, let him say how much he enjoyed your letter. Your taste and sensibilities have brightened his day. Yes, there is justice in the world. What is is right; all that it could be, given the conditions leading to it. Uncle Mike is, evidently, syndicated to the breaking point of the world's interest in his opinions. He's shocked things have gone as far as they have.

The plumping of America will come as no surprise to historians, of whom one of the more snotty will suggest the motto on our currency should have read, In Ourselves We Indulge. The plagues threatening, and snickering at, twentieth century America are self indulgence and its idiot twin, self-righteousness. Americans spend more on dieting than the United Nations spends on famine relief and throw away as much as the rest of humanity consumes. From this podium, we counsel the world on what it should do with its life.

We're fat for the same reasons we're overextended on credit: the people with something to sell have convinced us that self control, not to mention anything as drastic as good old fashioned restraint, are a sin against our national birthright. We feel we owe ourselves a luxury four wheel drive personal assault vehicle for the same reason we deserve meals that would feed third world families for a week: because we're number one. There's a fine, fatal line between freedom and license and our culture is hell bent on erasing it.

Will overweight women become the beauty norm? All things are possible, some are worth dying to prevent. Will male paunches become power symbols? Unless shedding blubber becomes tax deductible and moderation becomes a marketable virtue, probably yes.

• • •

147

Dear Uncle Mike,

I am a twelve year old girl. My teacher asked us to write about men and women, whether they're different or not and how much and what way and if they're equal. I asked a lot of people and read about it but could you tell me? If it was in your column I could get a better grade too.

Chris T., Seattle, Washington

Dear Chris,

As you and Uncle Mike both know, girls are different from boys; men and women even more so. This will be true if a female basketball player becomes a five time MVP in the NBA and the CEOs of the top five Fortune 500 corporations aren't men. The difference between men and women is biological. It's not just that women can bear children and men can't; it's that their body chemistries exist to fulfill one reproductive function or another. Body chemistry determines our thoughts and perceptions, our moods, our drives and, to a large extent, our individual destinies. Female hormones aren't male hormones and they never will be. It's said that society creates gender differences. Uncle Mike thinks gender differences create society. Rather than competing with each other, men and women should complement each other's power. If for no other reason than that the universe functions that way. At the bottom of anything that happens, something is either emitted or absorbed. Emission is not better than absorption, or stronger, or smarter. It's only different. And equal. After women understand what it means to be a woman and men understand what it means to be a man, we can all start learning what it means to be human. That's when the real fun starts.

• • •

Dear Uncle Mike,

Why do women start off wanting sex as much as the guy but always wind up not wanting it as much? I'm starting to think women use sex just to hook you.

Chad S., Beaverton, Oregon

Dear Chad,

Although any woman with the brains God gave a crowbar knows the sexual power she wields over men, especially men like you, only a woman without the brains God gave a crowbar would use it to 'hook' one, especially one like you. At the risk of spitting into the wind, he'll try to explain the situation in words you can understand. Women, following the advice of their DNA, have sex (for the most part) with men who make them feel loved and secure. That they can be fooled explains why men like you have a sex life at all.

• • •

Dear Uncle Mike,

      Care to comment on the Men's Movement?
                        Snicker-Chuckle, Tempe, Arizona

Dear Ms. Chuckle,

Being hopelessly out of the loop, Uncle Mike was unaware that men were moving. It's probably for the best. The neighbors were complaining. Maybe someday, after the wounds have healed, we can all get together for coffee and celebrate being human.

• • •

Dear Uncle Mike,

I'm thinking about seeing a counselor but I thought I'd write you first. I'm twenty-eight and have been married for two years. My husband is thirty-three. He is a good man and I love him but I'm worried he may be a sex addict. I enjoy sex myself but some nights I'd just rather not. If we don't have sex at least five times a week, my husband starts asking me if something's wrong. I don't think there's anything wrong with me. A friend gave me a book on sexual addiction and a lot of the things it said fit my husband. He likes adult videos, buys me fantasy underwear, and wants sex at inappropriate times. He doesn't think he has a problem and says

149

he's just a very sexual person. He tries to be sensitive but that just makes it worse because I start thinking it's me who's being insensitive. It's not a huge problem yet but it could be. I'd be interested in any thoughts you have. Do you answer questions you don't use in your columns?

Name Withheld, Portland, Oregon

Dear Person,

Popular psychology is popular because of its ability to uncover rich seams of abnormality in people we thought were normal, ourselves included. Like the ferreting out of witches, it can become socially addictive. Uncle Mike has no idea which book your friend loaned you but he strongly suggests you return it. Given that most men think about sex several hundred times a day, he doubts that a thirty-three year old male who wants sex five times a week needs to be trussed up and shuffled off to a treatment center.

A good working definition of addiction is any behavior that a) damages yourself, b) damages your relationships with others, or c) interferes with your work. For a man your husband's age, frequent sex should pose no personal risk. Since you didn't mention it, Uncle Mike assumes he doesn't watch naughty movies on the job or embarrass himself by rubbing up against the coat rack in the presence of his coworkers. This brings us to relationships. Does your husband have any? Do they seem reasonably successful? Does he have friends with whom he's not having sex? Are any of them women? As regards *your* relationship, does his interest in you ever stray beyond the carnal? Does he seem to regard you as a human being? Are his advances such that you need to fend him off with a cattle prod?

If the fact that your husband enjoys watching videotapes of sexual acts between consenting actors indicates pathology, your book will surely have addressed the fact that, according to industry figures, some thirty percent of adult movies are rented by women; at least some of whom must not be sex addicts. That your husband buys you the sort of lingerie that qualifies as gift-wrap is also hopelessly normal. Or at least within the bounds of a society that includes the Victoria's Secret catalogue. As for your husband wanting sex at 'inappropriate' times, Uncle Mike would need more information in order to comment; except to say that anything that frightens the horses is definitely a bad idea. Reduced to first principles, which is to say the state it was in before you read about what it might be, your problem boils down to your husband wanting sex more often than you. Forgive him. The poor slob is young and in love and, pitifully strung out on testosterone, probably thinks he arouses you as much as you arouse him. Have faith that your attitude and his bitter experience will change things. Hopefully, it will take the form of a compromise between two people who love and respect each other.

. . .

Dear Uncle Mike,

I have been friends with a woman for almost fifteen years. During that time, we have both been in various relationships, never single at the same time. We're not now either. I'm not involved but she has been married for several years. We've always been very attracted to each other but, aside from an occasional hug that lasted too long, we've never done anything about it. Neither of us are getting any younger and we're considering just going ahead and doing it. She has no intention of leaving her husband and neither of us want to hurt anyone. We just want to complete our friendship. I know it qualifies as cheating but as long as I'm not breaking up a marriage, I don't know if I think it's all that wrong. I could use your thoughts.

D.L., Seattle, Washington

Dear D.L.,

What you need is a brain. Repeat after Uncle Mike: there is no such thing as casual sex among thinking people, especially if one of them is a woman. You are about to have a former close friend. If either of you has a more developed sense of ethics than a weasel in heat, you'll do the other one a favor by reminding them of life's best piece of advice: doing unto others in ways you'd like to be done unto. Since you didn't mention any special under-standing between your friend and her husband, Uncle Mike must assume that, regardless what you call it, he would see the two of

151

you sleeping together as a violation of social contract. Of course, he'll never find out because your story is different than the thousands of movies built on similar plots. His ignorance, even if it should remain intact, will still not guarantee your bliss. Do this thing and you and your friend will never look at yourselves with the sort of pride and respect that make friendship possible. Unless, of course, you're not the kind of people who have pride and respect. Or the kind who believe that what goes round comes round.

· · ·

Dear Uncle Mike,

I recently met a man who is as nearly perfect as he can be. Kind, attentive, honest, intelligent, possessed of a good sense of humor, and successful in his profession. We've been seeing each other steadily for eight months and I've fallen very much in love with him. Two weeks ago, he proposed marriage. I accepted without reservation. Two nights ago, we went out to dinner and he handed me a preliminary draft of a prenuptial agreement. I was flabbergasted. I knew such things existed but I never imagined I'd see one. Basically, what it says is that if the marriage is unsuccessful, each of us takes with us what we brought to it, plus half of whatever we accumulate together. I'm buying a modest home and have an IRA and a few thousand dollars in savings. He owns his home and has substantial assets of various sorts. He says the agreement is simply a reflection of our shared sense of fairness but does admit that after being taken to the cleaners by his first wife, he would rather not depend entirely on good intentions. This has had a chilling effect on me. It would never occur to me to take things that weren't mine regardless how much ill will existed in case of divorce. I resent that he does not have faith in me. We've spoken several times since about this and he remains firm, saying that if worse comes to worst, it will eliminate unpleasantness between us and the possibility of large legal fees. I'm 32 years old and consider myself fairly sophisticated but this is just not my idea of approaching a commitment. He's 41 and believes it's the only way for intelligent people to enter into a shared life. I'd be interested to know what you think.

Wrestling With Principle, Beaverton, Oregon

Dear Wrestling,

Uncle Mike thinks you and your fiancé are ill-suited. In his experience, people either love people more than they love things or they love things more than they love people. There's nothing inherently wrong with either approach (many paths, one mountain), but it's one of those fundamental differences that are either reconcilable or not. As you've mentioned, the issue isn't money, it's trust. And faith. The failings we notice first in other people are the ones we suffer from ourselves. If your life partner to be feels the need to hedge his bet, it means he's at least as unsure of his definition of for better and worse as he is of yours. Like you, Uncle Mike has seen enough of life to know that divorce happens to the best intentioned couples and that matters can turn ugly when it's time to divide up the pots and pans. Still, once again like you, he sees prenuptial agreements as a combination of self fulfilling prophecy and planned obsolescence. Marriage is not a business venture. It is, or jolly well should be, a merging of souls; a leap of faith as opposed to a merging of assets. Neither is love a rational act. It's a state of fulfilling and being fulfilled, an act of unity made holy by the spirit of abandon. Why, the naive romantic in Uncle Mike must ask, would anyone want to marry someone they didn't trust? The function of contracts is to clarify conditions and minimize risks. The function of love is to accept risk as an acceptable condition. Perhaps, if Uncle Mike were a rich man who'd been taken to the cleaners, he'd feel differently. He certainly hopes not.

As for you, Uncle Mike would recommend you not fall victim to your fiancé's love of 'stuff' by overreacting to his woeful insecurities. If you love the man and truly want to spend the rest of your life with him; and if the agreement is, as it seems to be, nothing more than a reflection of your own sense of fairness; and if the mere mention of contracts hasn't irrevocably shattered your faith in his capacity to love, then sign the stupid thing. If, as it sounds from your letter, you're having serious second thoughts, honor them. Tell the man you never mix business with pleasure and that, if making love isn't enough of a handshake for him, marriage would only lead to pain and sadness.

• • •

Dear Uncle Mike,

    I'm sixteen and my question is why do girls put up with boy-friends who treat them like (feces)? This girl I like is going out with a no good creep who cheats on her and lies about it and orders her around. My aunt's husband yells at her a lot and I think he hits her. Why do they stay with guys who don't respect them?

David S., Reno, Nevada

Dear David,

    People, both men and women, stay in abusive relationships because they've been taught to expect abuse and to believe they deserve it. People for whom abuse is normal tend to meet people who'll abuse them and people who abuse others always find people willing to accept abuse. It's an odd world. Girls and women also have a fascination with outlaws: boys and men whose power is based on the rejection of authority. Rejecting authority is a good thing, little in history having been accomplished by those who were content to color inside the lines. What often seems unclear to the ladies is the huge difference between an outlaw and a criminal. Hopefully, your young lady will learn the difference sooner rather than later and your aunt will learn it as soon as she can. The first rule of any civilization has to be that nobody hits anyone. Ever.

• • •

Dear Uncle Mike,

    My ex-writing instructor is gorgeous. He is also smart, funny, and did I mention gorgeous? I'm very frustrated because he ignores me. I call him sometimes just to hear his voice. I don't say anything. He loathes me, I think. He told me to leave him alone. I think we are meant to be together, in some context. Not necessarily romantic. How can I get him to change his mind about me? I fantasize about sending him anonymous love letters (or just letters) but I think he would know it was me. Please help. I challenge you to come up with an answer besides "Get over it".

Katherine, Kingman, Arizona

Dear Katherine,

Although Uncle Mike dearly loves ignoring challenges, in your case he'll rise to the bait. March yourself into the bathroom, look deeply into the mirror, and repeat after Uncle Mike: "I am exhibiting obsessive behavior." Not that there's anything wrong with obsession; there being precious little in the way of art and science that would have been created without it. It's just that, in order for anything to come of obsession, the obsessee has to know they're obsessing. The people at Webster's define obsession as "a persistent, disturbing preoccupation with an often unreasonable idea or feeling." This is, of course, a good working definition of falling in love. The notion of romantic love, as opposed to the merely glandular, comes to us from the middle ages, from the spiritual roots that flowered into knighthood: a tradition in which men wore armor so heavy that, should reality ever bring them to their knees, they were unable to get back up. (Uncle Mike senses a dandy doctoral thesis here but refuses to obsess about it.) For a knight, the purest love possible had, for its object, a lady whose favors were, for one reason or another, absolutely and irrevocably unattainable. Love without hope for return is a spiritual exercise of potent force. Unless, of course, you don't understand the drill, in which case you become an obsessed mope lusting for a result that never comes. Uncle Mike will leave it to you to decide which pole you're closer to. No, he won't. Given that this person has asked you to leave him alone, continuing to plan a future together, romantic or otherwise, is to indulge unreasonable ideas and feelings and operate as if they were reasonable. At best, you're being silly. Your silent phone calls qualify as harassment, an illegal behavior you should immediately decide is beneath you.

Uncle Mike suggests you meditate on the distinction between falling in love and rising to it. If there truly is a karmic link between you and your ex-teacher (a relationship chock full of lessons on the mutual abuse of power), it will unfold much more prettily if you exercise your love by wishing this man the best the universe has to offer. Love him from a distance, with neither the hope nor the intention of ever laying eyes on him again, let alone rekindling a never existent romance. Things are what they are and one of life's loveliest and most unsettling revelations is that whatever is, is right. Whatever the situation, it is, given all that led up to it, the only situation that could be. What happens may not always feel good but it's always impeccably appropriate. It sounds to Uncle Mike that, regardless how gorgeous and smart and funny this fellow is, what you're in love with is the idea of him, not the reality. His reality wants you to leave him alone. Uncle Mike recommends you get over it.

• • •

Dear Uncle Mike,

I'm a waitress and you earned my love a year or two ago when you said that if it doesn't fold, it's not a tip. I'm not going to go on about pay scales and taxes. I make a living and I'm not a whiner. I just would like to see people show a little courtesy and respect. The way customers treat service personnel has really changed in the last few years. Arrogance, rudeness, and attitude. A lot of people read your column and I was hoping you could spare a few words on 'table manners'.

Annie, Portland, Oregon

Dear Annie,

Uncle Mike leaps at the chance. People dine out, to experience what life would be like with staff. Some of them confuse staff with indentured servants and imagine they're paying for the privilege to be the sort of boorish louts whose staff would rise up and murder them with mallets. For reasons known only to themselves, they believe that the ability to subcontract a meal grants them a license to complain about nothing, send back to the kitchen food they couldn't prepare if their lives depended on it. They were somehow allowed to grow up without learning that service is the holiest of vocations and that the oldest ritual of any society is that of the guest and the host.

In terms able to be understood by those who wouldn't know class behavior if the instructions were printed on their platinum VISA: the person who brings your food and refills your cup is a full fledged human being whose life is only partially defined and fulfilled by serving you; his or her role is to bring you whatever you want, not to provide a vessel for your petty frustrations and smarmy urges to power; dining in public is a civilized activity and civilized people treat each other with honor and respect. Especially if the person you're treating can go back to the kitchen and do disgusting things with your pasta.

None of these considerations apply to servers who introduce themselves before being asked. At the first sign stop them with a firmly outstretched palm and say, "I'm truly sorry but I already know so many people that, until one of them dies or goes back to prison, I couldn't possibly meet anyone else." If they persist, douse them with your ice water and leave a smaller than usual tip.

· · ·

Dear Uncle Mike,

I'm angry because men never want to be friends with me. They want more and they act passive-aggressive and mean when that's all I want. My therapist says I have a fear of intimacy, but I think that's a crock of (poop). I just have very high standards and am content with friendship most of the time.

Eileen, Portland, Oregon

Dear Eileen,

Uncle Mike is sad to hear you're angry. So much of life demands clear thinking and thinking clearly while angry is every bit as challenging as meditating in a drum factory. Instead of railing against what is, Uncle Mike always counsels himself to accept it. The men you meet, or, more correctly, the men you've been meeting, don't want to be just friends with you. A quick glance through any number of popular magazines, or the first two thousand years of recorded history, will show you your problem is not unique. While men are quite capable of friendship, it's not usually the spirit that drives them when it comes to seeking out relationships with women. This is especially true if the men are young, which is to say, not yet house trained. Just as deeply and sincerely as you want a friend, these men want someone to have sex with. This is the fundamental dynamic between the genders that makes dancing together such a charming, intoxicating struggle.

157

Speaking scientifically, regardless how sensitive and caring post-liberation man might be, having a woman he's vividly pictured himself naked with tell him it's never going to happen can be a bitter pill to swallow. Older men are, as a rule, easier to deal with, having experienced enough pain and humiliation to get the point. Men, you must understand, take sexual rejection very personally. Unevolved beings that they are, they feel much the way you do when a man rejects your urge to spiritually bond. Being hurt can, as your letter makes plain, cause the best of people to react inappropriately.

As for whether you are or are not intimacy challenged (which would make you a victim and possibly allow you to sue your parents and everyone else who's ever harmed or frightened you for damages), you have, thank goodness, given Uncle Mike no clues to go on. He sincerely hopes you're able to be intimate whenever you darn well feel like it. That you don't often feel like it is between you and the universe. Unless your standards are high enough to isolate you from reality, refuse to lower them an inch. Your only responsibility is to be compassionate toward those men whose standards and good taste were high enough to include you.

• • •

Dear Uncle Mike,

I am a very shy person and people who say "smile!" make me angry. I am shy and serious and that is just who I am. I am sick and tired of people suspecting I'm dour and/or a snob. I'm not. Why can't I be accepted just the way I am?

       Erika, Bellingham, Washington

Dear Erika,

Uncle Mike hates to sound mean, but you are in fact being accepted just the way you are. The way you are, shy and serious, makes people nervous. Their first tendency is to fill in your perceived void with whatever conversational topic they come up with, usually themselves. If you don't respond to this, they may up the tempo to more animated performances, up to and including animal impersonations. One of the surest ways to induce a short circuit in the outgoing is to deny them feedback. In the right frame of mind, the shy and serious find it fascinating to watch. Unless you live in a basement apartment, have no television, and never venture out, you'll have noticed that the shy and serious are hilariously outnumbered by the boorish and shallow: a behavioral gene pool dubbed, by someone less kind than Uncle Mike, 'the many too many'. Nothing frightens the many too many more than someone who isn't like them; which is to say, like someone they've seen on television. Unless you are ready and willing to spend several minutes of the life that's left you discussing episodes of Seinfeld, swapping low level insights about Monica Lewinsky, or go endlessly on about money, the unforgivable faults of your mate, or the mileage achieved by your new personal assault vehicle, you're going to make people nervous. There's not a thing in the world wrong with this. If the universe didn't want them to feel threatened, you'd hardly be there for them.

. . .

Dear Uncle Mike,

What is the strangest sexual fantasy you've ever had? The most annoying thing about you? The stupidest thing you've ever done? Your most embarrassing moment? Come on, open up. You make fun of everyone else.

Shirley Jean, Prescott, Arizona

Dear Shirley Jean,

Like others before you, you've misunderstood the nature of the column. If Uncle Mike wished to be the subject of inquiry, he would have called it Meet Uncle Mike. However, since you were rude enough to ask, Uncle Mike is polite enough to answer as honestly as he wants to. Your first question is impossible to answer since Uncle Mike's naughty fantasies are his own business. Except for the one with the seals, which is, to no one's great joy, a matter of public record. The most annoying thing about Uncle Mike would have to be either the harmonica or the late night barking. Uncle Mike has never done a stupid thing in his life. He has, of course, done many things without knowing he was cleverly setting himself up to learn an especially brutal lesson. Many of these lessons have involved interesting women, sour mash whiskey, and the writing of bad checks. He is, of course, much better now. Of the many embarrassing moments Uncle Mike has put himself through, none compares to the week he spent trying to talk without using the word 'I' and discovering how much of his conversation had himself as its real subject.

• • •

Dear Uncle Mike,

I can't imagine asking Ann Landers for advice, but I will ask you. To be blunt, my eighteen year old daughter is dating a bum. It's not just that he spends most of his time sitting around drinking beer and smoking dope—my husband and I both did our share of that and we managed to grow up into thinking, responsible, creative people—it's that he's neither interested in nor thinks about anything. Nothing. Including buying his own beer. Our daughter is an intelligent young woman whose art has landed her a scholarship at a good university. She'll be going away to school in September and my worry is that this bum will follow her and continue to make a mess of her life. It really never occurred to my husband or I that our daughter would get mixed up with someone like this. I don't write to you for solutions, only insight.

A Mother, San Francisco

Dear Mom,

Thank you for writing. Uncle Mike is always cheered by notes from people who use neither and nor; even those who are surprised when their intelligent and artistic young daughter takes up with a bum. Uncle Mike reels at the thought of how many times this motif has appeared in literature, motion pictures and television, let alone in real life, and finds it charming that neither you nor your husband imagined it might become a subplot in yours. Owing to biochemical gender distinctions we're not allowed to talk about, women are fascinated with the notion of taming things, giving form to the formless, making wholes out of parts. Women seem, whether by nature or nurture, to be especially drawn to lonely men with bleeding emotional wounds: the outlaw motif Dylan refers to in the line, 'Come in, she said, I'll give you shelter from the storm.' As your daughter is sure to discover, some of the outlaws are in fact criminals and shouldn't be allowed in the house, let alone sheltered from any self induced storms.

Uncle Mike recommends that you and your husband renew your faith in your child. It's a long game and, in the long run, the patterns she weaves in her life will be those she learned from you. If her father didn't spend her childhood swilling beer and ignoring anything that passed for thought, neither will the partner she winds up with. Between now and then, of course, all hell can break loose. Your daughter is poised on the slippery edge of an adventure you'll never know the half of and you're best off trusting she knows which end of the oar to put in the water. Since intelligent and artistic young women draw interesting and promising young men like ball bearings to a magnet, Uncle Mike would bet his lava lamp she'll find someone in one of her classes that puts her current drone into harsh perspective. With any luck, he won't be worse.

You could, of course, just to hedge your bet, have your husband draw the lout aside and explain, man to boy, the very real hazards he could face should he decide to move to the same city as your daughter. A nonpaternal pat on the cheek will drive the point home nicely.

• • •

Dear Uncle Mike,
I have this friend who communicates with me psychically. I'd like to strengthen the connection but don't know how. Any suggestions?

Mary, Tempe, Arizona

Dear Mary,
All magic, which is to say that portion of experience not explained by science, depends upon will and intent. Psychic bonds, like muscles, gain strength through exercise. Given this, your question becomes, how do I get to Carnegie Hall?, to which the only answer is, practice.

• • •

Dear Uncle Mike,

I read somewhere about these psychologists who study happiness. According to their statistics, about 98% of Americans are happy. I say they only think they are and or the studies are flawed. What do you say?

Robert, Portland, Oregon

Dear Robert,

Pardon Uncle Mike while he snorts. Wherever these psychiatrists gathered their sample, it wasn't anywhere Uncle Mike has been recently. We could, of course, be dealing with an ill defined term. For a culture trained not to recognize the difference between pleasure and mindless excitement, the term 'happiness' becomes as vague as 'love'. We also need to remember, even if the psychiatrists don't, that happiness is a success object. To be unhappy is thus to be unsuccessful, and so, second rate and flawed. Uncle Mike has no problem accepting that 98% of the sampling would write bad checks before putting themselves in that category. While this represents a level of denial bordering on delusion, matters could be worse. Ninety-eight percent of us could be unhappy and spend our lives expecting someone else to do something about it.

• • •

Dear Uncle Mike,

Do you have any books that have changed your life?

Marta, Portland, Oregon

Dear Marta,

You bet.

• • •

Dear Uncle Mike,

What is the best way to impress a man? (I'm a woman.)

Jean, Elko, Nevada

Dear Jean,

As Uncle Mike prays you've discovered, it depends on the man you're talking about. The problem is that many men are actually postgraduate boys and, therefore, most easily impressed by women who'll have sex with them and, without meddling in their affairs, take care of them the way they always thought their mother should have. Unless everyone's on the same page, it can be an ugly, confusing business. For the sake of not having to speak of such things, let's assume the man you're talking about is, in spite of the near lethal levels of testosterone coursing thorough his system, a grownup; which is to say, a fully operational male human. (FOMs are, like FOFs, rare as hen's teeth; so rare sociologists worry about their chances of finding each other to mate.) Full blown humans of any gender are impressed by honesty, compassion, loyalty, some form of native intelligence, and the ability to laugh. Although we now know there is absolutely no difference between men and women, women are attracted to will and power and men are suckers for grace and beauty, especially if they think there's a chance of having sex with it. The most any of us can do is be the best possible version of ourselves and see who it impresses. You might try not caring. Not only will it free up the sort of energy that makes a person impressive, we're all attracted to mystery. We're also all lonely, frightened and filled with serious doubts we measure up. For the magic to work, the people performing it must be friends. There's nothing more impressive than someone who knows how to be one, and nothing worth bothering with less than someone who's not impressed by it. Or at least flattered. Uncle Mike has seen grown men stripped of their senses by someone they wanted to have sex with compliment their tie. It's a funny world.

. . .

163

Dear Uncle Mike,

My sister has a three year old son who exposes himself to company. It wasn't cute when he started doing it two months ago and it's not cute now. She and her husband—he's not the child's father—have tried everything. Telling him it's not nice, swatting his butt, putting him in his room. It's to the point now they're going to take him to a sitter's when they have company. My question is, is this normal? I have a two year old daughter and they play together all the time. Do normal three year old boys drop their pants in front of people? I know there are a lot of theories but sometimes I think you're right on and I'd like you to answer.

Little Sister, Astoria, Oregon

Dear Sister,

Normal is a very interesting word, best used in contexts such as 'normal wear and tear', 'normal vital signs', and 'normal recycling days'. Applied to human behavior, it would mean that Van Gogh might have been helped with Prozac. Much pain and sadness can be prevented by adopting the notion of 'appropriate'. Is your nephew's behavior inappropriate? Goodness yes. Should something be done to stop it? It certainly would if he did it in Uncle Mike's house. There is no unified theory of child psychology because there are no unified theoretical children. They are reflecting mirrors of what the world has shown them. Happy children have seen happiness, polite children have seen courtesy, compassionate children have felt love. No, this doesn't mean, at least not necessarily, that, when no one is around, your sister and her husband run around the ranch house flashing each other. In and of itself, it probably has no meaning. Uncle Mike would suggest reducing the child to first principles. What young Rudolph (let's call him that, just for fun) is doing is getting attention. He could have done any number of things to get it: crying, screaming, crawling into someone's lap and putting his nose against theirs. None of those behaviors would have been the point either. The point is that young Rudolph is either a) not getting enough attention, or b) not getting the right sort of attention. Having the great good fortune not to know your sister, her husband who's not the child's father, and young Rudolph, Uncle Mike will allow all of you to sort that out. As far as Rudolph's inappropriate, insufferable, and obnoxious behavior, many such asocial outbursts can be short circuited by the first rule of parenting: be one step ahead of the child. At the first sign young Rudy's feeling neglected enough to drop his pants, the complete parent will, perhaps with a merry laugh, scoop the child up in his or her arms and waltz it into its bedroom where, in quiet security, the apprentice human can have enough undivided attention to decide whether it wants to be with civilized people or not. Uncle Mike heard a lovely story once about a tribe of American primitives who would, when a child was fussing for no reason other than to hear itself fuss, hang its carrier on a tree branch near enough for it to be part of things without being heard. This is, of course, child abuse, and Uncle Mike would never recommend actually suspending Rudolph from a hook on the front porch. The hook should be a sturdy one and his favorite pillow placed beneath him should his struggles become a lesson in cause and effect.

· · ·

Dear Uncle Mike,

My girlfriend and I broke up a month ago, we lived with each other for almost a year. We're both 27. The breakup was my idea. I love her but am not in love with her, I don't think I'm the man she needs and I don't want to be in a relationship right now. I really want us to be friends but she wants to get back together and I don't. What do you say?

Rian, Portland, Oregon

Dear Rian,

You say what we should always say: the truth. Uncle Mike assumes you've made your feelings clear; that, for the sake of kindness and cowardice, you've not given her any mixed signals about the future. If you're doing that, you should stop it. If the young woman is aware of how you feel and persists in tilting at your windmill, we can assume she's a tad unbalanced. She has, in terms of the spherical geometry of spacetime, lost her center. In a universe bursting into song all around her, she is feeling unloved and abandoned. As the friend you propose to be, Uncle Mike would suggest you do all you can to change that. If having a friendship without being partners is something she can't get her emotional and intellectual arms around, there's nothing to do but back away, be the best friend you can be, and give it time. Amazing medicine, time. Who knows? Your persistence in caring for her just might remind your friend what she already knows in her heart: that wanting what we can't have keeps us from getting what's ours. Then again, she could be a borderline whacko whose slim tether to reality has been severed by the ax of your unacceptable rejection. In which case, you'll need to move to another city and get a large dog.

• • •

Dear Uncle Mike,

I'm furious. Do you really think hanging fussy children from hooks on the front porch is something you should suggest to people? Even meant as a joke, it's in extremely poor taste. I don't plan to read your column again.

Furious, Elko, Nevada

Dear Furious,

Uncle Mike was going to suggest propping the little organism up in front of a video game but his knee jerk compassion stopped him. Integrating children into polite society is a long process demanding patience and forbearance on everyone's part; the child included. Learning patience and forbearance is, in fact, a large part of the teaching. Encouraging children to believe their need for attention takes precedent over whatever the rest of the world is doing is child abuse: no child should be allowed to reach puberty uncertain of the knowledge that, if you make a nuisance of yourself, nice people and pleasant events will avoid you. While Uncle Mike is beside himself at the thought of losing your attention, his inner child intends to pick up the pieces and soldier on.

• • •

Dear Uncle Mike,

My friend says that powerful men are submissive and/or masochistic in bed. She says they are this way because it is a relief and/or a way of balancing out. In my experience, <u>all</u> men are submissive and/or masochistic in bed. What has been your experience? You could ask a few female friends as well.

Love, Peggy, Kingman, Arizona

Dear Peggy,

In Uncle Mike's experience, which is to say those few times when another male slept within arm's reach, the men (some of whom were probably powerful or became powerful after Boy Scouts) were, by mutual agreement, standoffish and remote. As for asking a few female friends to tell me more than they already have about men, Uncle Mike can only mumble his excuses. It makes wonderful sense that the powerful of either gender, by way of letting their hair down, might welcome the opportunity, or even the command, to go with the flow. Uncle Mike has noticed that, in an absurd number of cases, people project what they truly are not. Powerful people gather power in order not to feel powerless; a process that rarely finds closure. The powerful are the world's needy and needy people accept submission as a fact of life. That, in your experience (the length and breadth of which Uncle Mike is contentedly ignorant of), <u>all</u> men are submissive and/or masochistic may well mean that you are the woman of their dreams. Someone to take control, kick rump if need be, anything to take them away. Which, of course, could mean that this take charge nursedominatrix gig is only the persona you project in order to meet powerful men whose compensating mechanisms recognize yours. As for Uncle Mike, not being the sort of person for whom 'powerful' is the first word that leaps to mind, he just comes to bed in a coonskin cap and bunny jammers and lets nature take its course..

• • •

Dear Uncle Mike,

    I read your column a lot and I like what you say about people's problems. Here's mine. I'm seventeen and my best friend stole my boyfriend. I couldn't believe it. Other friends told me stuff after that I didn't know. All the time she acted like my friend. I see them both a lot and it makes me mad and sad at the same time. How can people do this? How do you know before it happens?

                       Stephanie, Portland, Oregon

Dear Stephanie,

    Aside from actually being clairvoyant, the ability to know things before they happen is the result of spending a lot of time thinking about why things happen and testing your theories against actual human behavior. This process is called experience and comes with getting older. As long, that is, as the person getting older is also getting smarter. There are, it seems to Uncle Mike, two important things to remember while wallowing in your anger and pain. First, that your best friend was no friend at all; and second, that your boyfriend was not really your boyfriend. Had he been your boyfriend, when your best friend batted her eyes, he would have made his nonintentions clear and been reaffirmed and reborn in his love for you. He didn't do that. He went for it like a hungry trout. If your best friend had been any friend at all, she would have verbally cut him to the navel at the first sign of inappropriate behavior or unethical intent. She didn't do that either.

    When people have done things like this to Uncle Mike, he tries to remember two things. First, that he's been playing with people who have the moral code of diseased weasels. Second, that their loss should not, if he's thinking clearly, leave a big hole in his life. They may be the embodied spirits of a universe whose ultimate truth is the unity of all things, but they're behaving like scum bags and there's nothing that says you must stand around and smile at their low rent antics. Distance yourself from them and the feelings they encourage in you. Anger and sadness are toxic imbalances in your brain chemistry and, as chemical states, they can keep you from noticing opportunities to feel good. Then you're in a real pickle.

    Which brings us to the very real and necessary fun involved

in your second question: how can people do this? Understanding not only makes life more interesting, it's also the only antidote to pain and sadness; carried far enough, it always leads to compassion. One of the most charming, and most frightening, things about people is that, given the cards they've been dealt, they are, at each and every moment, doing the best they can. Once you realize the sort of fear and loneliness it would take to emotionally gut someone who trusted you, it's hard not to say, poor babies, and hope something happens soon to make them feel all better.

• • •

Dear Uncle Mike,

I've watched her show and I think there's something psychologically wrong with Martha Stewart. What do you think?

Elizabeth, Portland, Oregon

Dear Elizabeth,

Uncle Mike suspects there's something psychologically wrong with all of us. Since he doesn't know Martha (who, now that you mention it, does seem a little tightly wrapped), Uncle Mike would feel like a cad speculating on which colors are missing from her paint box. He will say that, if he and Martha were forced to winter together in any cabin smaller than Wrigley Field, there's a good chance only one of them would come out in the spring. Of course, Uncle Mike feels this way about a lot of people. It gives him the sort of charm that leads to the long periods of solitude necessary to advise others on their difficulties relating to the world around them. There may be something psychologically wrong with this. If so, it has yet to drive Uncle Mike to fuss over place settings for his poker support group.

• • •

Dear Uncle Mike,
> Are you a feminist?
>> Becky, Seattle, Washington

Dear Becky,
> Uncle Mike is a humanist who's comfortable with the notion of different but equal. If, by feminist, you mean someone who believes in equal pay for equal work and the sanctity of reproductive rights, Uncle Mike makes the cut. If you mean someone who, either through the assigning of blame or the acceptance of guilt, buys into the utter rot that women can only raise their consciousness by demeaning and belittling men and holding them personally and collectively responsible for whatever is wrong with their lives, then no, Uncle Mike is either, depending upon who's doing the labeling, a sexist swine or a knee jerk masculinist.

• • •

Dear Uncle Mike,
> I have a huge dilemma. I just got back together with an ex-boyfriend of six months. I am completely in love with him, and I am completely happy. The problem is, my parents don't like him. In fact, they hate him. This is because of some mistakes we made when we were together the first time. Both of us have grown up a lot, and learned from these mistakes. My question is should I keep seeing him and not tell my parents? Or, tell them and risk being confined to the house for the rest of my life? Please don't use my name. Thanks!!
>> Anonymous in Cyberspace

Dear Anonymous,
> You're quite welcome. There are two bits of information Uncle Mike can't help wishing you'd included: your age, and the nature of the 'mistakes' you and your friend made. If, for instance, you're both under eighteen and the mistakes involved missed curfews, a wild party or two, and being caught necking on the couch, Uncle Mike's response would be different than, say, if you're in your

twenties, still sucking free room and board while treating your parents like inn keepers, and your collective poor judgment embraced crime sprees or large civil suits.

You sound like an intelligent young woman so Uncle Mike will assume you and your young man are something at least vaguely resembling Romeo and Juliet: star crossed lovers scorned and beaten by a world that doesn't understand. First off, you mustn't dismiss the possibility that the world does understand and that it's you who's being self destructive and dumb as a post. There is, after all, a reason that 'love is blind' is a cliché'. But enough negativity. It's important to remember that, right or wrong, your parents are act- ing with what they perceive to be your best interests in mind. (Unless, of course, they actually are mindless, pathologically over- protective tyrants who wouldn't know true love if it bit them on the ankle and handed them a business card.) You've given them reason to believe that the chemistry between you two is not just intoxicating but toxic. Although that was then and this is now, your current behavior does nothing to weaken their case. You are, in the name of love, violating the trust of people who love you. This is not, as they say, a path with heart.

And so, happily enough, we discover your situation falls short of full blown dilemma. A dilemma implies a choice between equally awful alternatives, a situation with no satisfactory conclusion. Your choice is whether or not to act with integrity and its satisfactory outcome is that you stop living a lie. Yes, you need to tell your parents that you and he-who-can't-be-mentioned are once again an item. Tell them your respect for them made it impossible for you to continue sneaking behind their backs, and that you hope their respect for you is great enough to allow the two of you a second chance. If your friend has not, sincerely and face to face, apologized to your parents and asked their forgiveness for his displays of irresponsibility, he should do so; and, just as sincerely, vow that nothing of the sort will ever happen again. They're either going to believe him or not. Be optimistic. People can usually tell when someone is speaking the truth. If they still think the lad is pond scum and forbid you from seeing him, your decision still falls short of dilemma: you either continue to live at home or you make other arrangements. What could be more simple? If you decide against legal emancipation, tell your friend you can't continue to dishonor yourself by deceiving your parents while living under their roof. If he's the young man your parents don't think he is, he'll understand and the two of you will love each all the more desperately. Uncle Mike suggests you do it from a distance until your ceaseless, well reasoned nagging changes your parent's minds.

In the meantime, while you're locked in your attic room, gnawing on your pillow and cursing fate, remember it's more important to understand than it is to be understood; and that, if you're really looking for a dilemma, try behaving in ways you know are beneath you.

• • •

Dear Uncle Mike,

My wife and I have been married for 23 years and are still very happy together. We're the best of friends and sex is still great. In fact, it's better now than it was when we were in our 20s. Our younger friends call us compulsively monogamous and make fun of us. We've been pretty well ostracized from most social circles. What should we do?

Jim, Somewhere on the Web

Dear Jim,

As anyone familiar with self-help can tell you, and will if you don't jam a large cork in their mouth, the first step in any healing process is to admit you're the victim of a sick relationship. It's good you've cried out for help.

Repeat after Uncle Mike: My wife and I only think we're happy. We're actually in deep denial. Our friendship is an enabling mechanism that encourages us to ignore our self interests. Our sex is great only because we have nothing to compare it to. Life doesn't have to be this way.

Test the depth of your so called happy marriage by actively seeking small faults in each other from which to deduce major character flaws. Cut each other no slack. Seek the vision of The Ideal Mate and see just how well this person you 'love' stacks up against your imagination. Not a perfect match, is it? Go to separate bars and dwell on this. If perfection isn't attainable, would a nice universe make us want it? And if we want it, does this not mean we deserve it? And if we deserve it and don't have it, mightn't it be because someone very close to us is standing in our way, stifling our fulfillment with their love and loyalty? Can such a person truly be our friend? A few months of doubt and cynicism will whittle your marriage into something socially acceptable; which is to say, something more closely resembling the fun everyone has on *Dawson Creek*.

Aside from this, your only alternative is to resign yourselves to confinement in a fool's paradise. Uncle Mike congratulates you both and sincerely hopes you have children.

• • •

Dear Uncle Mike,

I am the REAL Uncle Mike. I have lots of great nieces (sic) and nephews lined up to testify to it. If you don't cease and desist, I'm afraid I'll have to ask my attorney (Hound from Hell) to send you one of those nasty lawyer letters.
                                    Uncle Mike, bordhead.net
P.S. Although I don't have a copyright, I do have a nice fax machine.

Dear Uncle Mike,

While Uncle Mike is happy you don't have a copyright, he's even happier you have a fax machine. For a person with your sort of personality disorder, it must be an indispensable tool. As for ceasing and desisting, let Uncle Mike assure you that yet another nasty letter from yet another nasty attorney will hardly bring him to his knees. He can, of course, be bought off; by some standards, rather cheaply.

• • •

Dear Uncle Mike,

I recently broke up with my boyfriend of two years. That's fine. He and I had some great times, but we hadn't been really happy for a long time. His needs outweighed my devotion, and his insecurity and lack of self-esteem were driving me batty.

The reason I'm writing you is that my best friend predicted that my boyfriend would be too needy, and that I would end up feeling as though he were sucking my life away, which is exactly what happened. The prediction actually came from a Ouija board, but my friend was co-piloting it, and I'm very familiar with her strong and accurate intuition and psychic abilities. Now I'm wondering if I shouldn't just let her pick out my next boyfriend for me. Or maybe I should never mention guys to her again, to prevent her from planting a seed of doubt in my mind.

How can I deal with this psychic friend? I love her dearly, and I know she has my best interests at heart, but it makes me feel lousy to know that her intuition about my relationship was superior to my own. How can I trust myself? Thank you.

Karen, Portland, Oregon

Dear Karen,

You're perfectly welcome. First off, allow Uncle Mike to say this: anyone who describes a relationship as having driven them 'batty' instead of unfairly victimizing them will have few inter-personal problems whose solutions can't be found hiding in plain sight.

You raise several questions. For the sake of brevity, let's not consider the Ouija board which, no matter how spookily accurate, will never hold a candle to the I Ching, one of whose teachings is that the end of things is always there at the beginning.

You use the terms 'devotion' and 'sucking my life away' to describe your experience with a person who was 'too needy' and riddled with 'insecurity and lack of self esteem'. You'll pardon Uncle Mike if he doesn't swoon from surprise. Self possessed, compassionate people attract the insecure and needy like iron filings to a magnet. As children are drawn to those who will mother them, the wounded and lame are drawn to those they hope can heal them. As a person of your qualities is bound to be aware, the attraction is mutual and based on the simplest of equations: those who have the most give to those with the least. Since we're all sick and lame in one way or another, much of the attraction we feel for each other springs from the urge to be nourished and made whole. The trick, as usual, lies in balance. The badly unbalanced imagine another human being is the only antidote to a poison they've taken. Close relationships with these people rarely work out. With practice, you'll learn where, and when, to draw that line in the sand that says, this far and no further. You'll get good, or at least better, at recognizing those who need more than they can give; and, with a little thought, you'll become better acquainted with you own need to nourish and be needed. The red lights on your control panel have always been there flashing, you'll just start noticing them sooner; and, before your hormones kidnap your good sense, adjusting your energies accordingly. Uncle Mike calls this process establishing the rules of engagement, the first one being: know when to disengage.

Which brings us, just when you thought Uncle Mike had forgotten what it was, to your original question: how best to deal with a friend who can read you like a cheap novel. Unless the woman goes on and on about your abysmal taste in men and seems too fond of the phrase 'I told you so', she sounds like a valuable ally. Uncle Mike would, nonetheless, advise against asking her to choose your next partner, as this will only detract from the fun. Since we learn more from our mistakes than we do from our successes, there's really no way to lose. Romance, like the rest of the human comedy, boils down to a game of poker: it's not just what you're dealt, it's how you play your cards. Uncle Mike hates when he sounds like a bumper sticker.

• • •

Dear Uncle Mike,
Does it ever bother you that you might be wrong and give somebody seriously bad advice? Don't get me wrong, I like your column (mostly). I'm just curious if you ever think about it.
Lisa, Eugene, Oregon

Dear Lisa,
    In all honesty, yes and no.

. . .

Dear Uncle Mike,
    Is it possible to love two people at the same time?
                                C.S., Salem, Oregon

Dear C.,
    Certainly. It's just not possible to explain it to either one of them.

. . .

Dear Sir:
    I refuse to call you Uncle Mike. In response to a recent letter you had the unmitigated gall to imply there is no blame and should be no guilt in the abusive and repressive society in which women find themselves. How dare you. It is not "utter rot" for women to demean and belittle those males who administer a physical and personal power system in which women remain either objects or support personnel. Men may not be responsible for all that is wrong in women's lives, just the worst of it. If I can help you with your labeling problem: you're neither a sexist swine, nor a knee jerk masculinist. You're just another (colloquial term for anus).
                                Former Reader, Seattle, Washington

Dear Former Reader,
    Uncle Mike is sad you're not having a good day and even sadder to think he might have helped it along. He's just glad it's a misunderstanding. Uncle Mike is well aware there are men, many too many of them, who compare badly to mindless brutes; and that there are many more who are only jerks with minds, money, and cultivated manners. Uncle Mike recommends that all women ignore them as religiously as he avoids both them and their sisters in spirit. (Of the many things that are gender specific, predatory and usurious behavior aren't among them.)

As for the male dominated power system at large, Uncle Mike shares your urge to throw up. Fortunately, once you realize it was designed, not to keep women in their place, but to grind up the poor and powerless of both sexes and feed them to the rich, issues of gender blend into the background of a rich tapestry of human rights abuse that is, viewed in the right spirit, an impressive piece of work.

Like you, Uncle Mike would love to see the machinery of greed and oppression dismantled and replaced with a garden devoted to the flowering of the human spirit. Unlike you, he has serious doubts it will flower any sooner if women and men, the two necessary components to the only system stronger than a global corporation, would rather take turns gutting each other than practice compassion, understanding, and love. Virtue is the only power available to the peasants; virtue and strength in numbers. The war is over when we want it to be. This brings us to 'personal responsibility': a much neglected chapter in the current annals of self-help.

Responsibility is, or was, the act of accepting ownership of the effects caused by our actions; a part of what used to be called 'character' in the days before we all realized we were 'victims'. Responsibility is based on the assumption that we're all on different paths, probably on the same mountain, and that each of us makes up our own path as we go along. We choose our way depending on where we've been, where we think we're going or, too often, what we had for lunch. Every path eventually teaches us that free will doesn't come cheap. Wherever we are, we're there because we decided to be, or because we let someone else decide for us, which is the same thing only worse. The first step to illumination is not to kneecap the last cheap punk who mugged your potential; it's copping to the fact that our lives are the exact products of the decisions we've made. It's we who've kept questionable company, we who've loved unwisely, we who've made poor use of our time, we who've squandered opportunities, we who still haven't learned the difference between pearls and pea gravel. Embarrassing, but there it is.

Regardless which bathroom fate has assigned him, if Uncle Mike exercises poor judgment, he expects the universe to deliver a lesson in the form of the mess he's whistled for. Whatever happens is the only thing that could have happened, given what came before, and the end of things is always in the beginning. It's hard to imagine a system any simpler or more fair, or one less likely to produce victims. Yes, there are huge, impersonal forces that work against us; but if we choose to arrange our lives so that, were we watching our little comedy from the audience, we'd spill our buttered popcorn screaming, "Grow a brain, you idiot!", how much blame is there left to lay at the feet of others? And, more importantly, isn't there something more constructive and fun we could be doing with our time?

It's easy for Uncle Mike to say this, of course. Being a man, he's in the driver's seat, king of all he surveys. The sound you hear is Uncle Mike slapping his knee and snorting.

• • •

Dear Uncle Mike,

I've been reading your column for some time now and unless you're so ugly you frighten children I want you. You're like way cool. You have my phone number. Use it.

Lynne, Reno, Nevada

Dear Lynne,

Uncle Mike's heart soars like an eagle to hear of your unhealthy obsession. As soon as he gnaws through his straps he'll try to get to a phone. Lucky you, Uncle Mike is far from ugly. Especially in his bunny pajamas.

• • •

Dear Uncle Mike,

How old do you think someone should be before they have sex? I'm sixteen and I'm definitely thinking about it. I want your opinion not your advice. I'll do what I decide to anyway. How old were you? P.S. I like your column. You have a mind.

J.J., e-mail

Dear J.J.,

Uncle Mike is glad you like his column and even gladder he has a mind. He finds it very handy when his emotions need talking to. It's good you didn't tell Uncle Mike your gender. He'd be willing to bet whatever's in the pot you're a young woman. Young men don't usually ask how old they should be to have sex, their attitude being that yesterday isn't soon enough. You ask Uncle Mike to resist giving advice. Thank you, Uncle Mike is happy for the break. As for opinions, everyone has one. There was an interesting study done recently at Ohio State University. Teenage girls who are sexually active are more likely to be depressed than those with no activity whatsoever. Sexually active teenage boys, on the other hand, are less likely to be depressed than those who are going out of their minds wanting to be, and less likely to have general feelings of failure. There's probably a message here. The researcher psychologists (Lori Kowaleski-Jones and Frank Mott) think it's this: "It seems like young girls who are not secure about themselves are seeking security and self-esteem through sexual relations. Meanwhile, teenage boys who are sexually active seem to be looking for sexual conquests or are oblivious to the implications of their behaviors." Even for adults, the play in the sandbox can get a little rough and a person always wants to make the best decision they can. As for your question about Uncle Mike's age when he first had sex, Uncle Mike can honestly say it's none of your business. He was, evidently, old enough. Unless you count the oblivious part.

. . .

Dear Uncle Mike,

The woman I'd been living with for a year broke up with me last month. I found out she'd been seeing the guy she's with now behind my back. She says they didn't sleep together but who knows. While we were together, her car broke down and I had the money so I bought her a new one. Not new, but not cheap either. Since she broke up with me, I think she should give it back. Let her new boyfriend buy her one. We don't talk so I wrote her a letter asking

about it and she didn't answer. The car is in her name so unless she gives it back, I'm out a couple thousand bucks and I'm _____ (colorful colloquial term having to do with the excreting of liquid waste). Should I get a lawyer or forget about it?
Dan, Beaverton, Oregon

Dear Dan,

Uncle Mike definitely thinks you should get a lawyer. People like you always need one eventually and there's no point putting things off. If, unlike you, the attorney you consult has a sense of ethics more developed than a puff adder, he'll tell you the car is hers, you don't have a leg to stand on, and charge you a large sum of money for listening to your whining. Uncle Mike wonders which part of the word 'gift' you find confusing and only hopes you didn't think you were buying something with it. Regardless whether or not your former friend behaved faithlessly, the car of the first part no longer has anything to do with you, just like the woman you mistook for someone else. To the observer, even one as disinterested as Uncle Mike, what you seem to be doing is blaming this someone else for a decision that you made. Regardless what your attorney says, this is not the act of a rational person.

· · ·

Dear Uncle Mike,

Do you think reality is observer determined?
Curious Reader, San Francisco

Dear Curious,

It depends. If we're talking about the macrocosm of karma (or its uglier twin, fate), Uncle Mike has no trouble accepting that what he did yesterday will have an effect on what happens today. Who he is and where he's been determine not just where he's going but much of what will happen when he gets there. He may not control all the variables, but he's certainly neither a blind pawn nor a thinking person's tumbleweed. In quantum terms, the world behind this one is a sea of unmanifest probabilities: all the things that could, given the circumstances, occur. Uncle Mike thinks of himself as a point conscious perspective; a perspective whose ancestors came over in the big bang. His history, or world line, has spent half of forever making him whatever he is and, at every point in the spacetime of his life, he brings this to the party. His mood, his expectations, his plans and dreams, his fears, his unresolved issues, his mistrust of cheese spread, his weakness for sultry brunettes. No matter where he goes, there he is, and the party is usually about as much fun as he's decided it will be. Is reality observer determined? Observer dependent would be closer. For any observer, reality is the intersection of his or her point conscious perspective with the point conscious perspectives of what's being observed. No, the trees Uncle Mike is looking at are not the trees you would see; and no, we can't put our toes in the same river even once.

. . .

Dear Uncle Mike,

This is a long story and it may sound weird. I've known this very special woman for five years. I fell in love with her the first time I saw her and we had an intense relationship for about a year before she moved to another city because of family obligations. We're both in our mid forties. We kept the relationship going for about a year, seeing each other every few months or so. The distance eventually won out. She started another relationship and so did I. Neither of them was good, mine ended, hers nearly has several times. I've been uninvolved for a few months now and haven't found anyone I'm interested in. I talk with my ex once or twice a month and I know she's not happy. We have an agreement not to bring up getting back together if either of us is involved, so I just listen and give her my opinion if she asks for it. She doesn't ask much. We've never stopped loving each other and I think in the back of my mind that I'm not finding anyone to get interested in because I think she's going to leave this person some day and I want to be here when she does. My best friend who knows both of us respects my loyalty and devotion but thinks I'm being stupid, that she could stay in an unhappy relationship for the rest of her life. I don't believe it.

Call Me Stupid, Eugene, Oregon

Dear Fellow Human,

On the basis of the information you've given him, Uncle Mike can't bring himself to call you stupid. Like your friend, he respects your loyalty and devotion; being a hopeless romantic himself, he's always cheered to see others living life as if it were a faerie tale. If dreams never came true, we'd hardly bother to remember them. Your approach seems to be rational: you've taken no public vow of celibacy, you haven't wrapped yourself in barbed wire, and you make no mention of purification rituals involving sharp objects or blunt instruments. You're merely weighing your options and separating the wheat from the chaff. Good man. Even should you decide consciously to save yourself for this woman, Uncle Mike wouldn't think you stupid; just patient and willing to spend large amounts of time being faithful to yourself: the ultimate, and most satisfying, form of monogamy. What you're doing, or seem to be doing, and certainly jolly well should be doing, is loving without lust for result: the purest of romantic traditions. You're either a man among men or a pitiful mope who doesn't know when to give up. This is, happily enough, a question only you and time can answer.

. . .

Dear Uncle Mike,

Have you ever wished you were a woman?
Chris, e-mail

Dear Chris,

Wondered many times, yes. Wished, no. Uncle Mike has enough on his plate trying to be himself and would bet large sums of money that, were he a woman, the work would only be different, not easier.

. . .

Dear Uncle Mike,

My eighteenth birthday is next month and instead of having a party my friends and I—about eight of us—want to go camping. Three guys are going. It was okay as long as it was just girls but now my parents are getting all weird. Only one of the guys is going with one of the girls, the other two are just friends who we all know. The one couple might sleep together but probably not and besides they have sex already anyway. The rest of us just want to go camping. My aunt who I like a lot is on my side. She suggested I write to you. You're an uncle, wouldn't you let your niece go camping for her birthday?

Holly, Portland, Oregon

Dear Holly,

Eight people is not camping. Eight people is bivouacking. Aside from what could easily turn into an assault on a forest, Uncle Mike thinks your idea of a birthday celebration is leagues ahead of pizza and a movie at the mall. With a few small reservations, you have Uncle Mike's blessings; and his prayers. Condition number one: at least three of the campers must have camped before and know which end of the hatchet to miss their hands and feet with. Condition number two: at least three of you must be sober at all times. Condition number three: those who don't cook wash the dishes. Condition number four: don't kill or hurt anything that was living and well when you found it. Condition number five: make sure when you leave, no one would know you were there. Happy birthday. Make your parents proud.

. . .

Dear Uncle Mike,

Is it just me or do you think telephone sex is a little weird? A couple of women I work with who aren't at all the type I'd think would be into it are. It seems a little silly and sad to me. Self gratification is one thing, talking through it with someone who isn't there is another. I think I'd start giggling and spoil the mood. You don't have to answer this in print if you don't want to. In fact, you don't have to answer it at all.

Sherri, Portland, Oregon

Dear Sherri,

For his own peace of mind, Uncle Mike long ago stopped regarding any form of sex between consenting adults of the same species as weird. This said, he shares your difficulty relating to the telephone as a marital aid. He fears that, long before the helpless laughter started, he'd have run out of exciting, or even clever, things to say. More fun would be a leisurely discussion of the meaning of telephone sex in the context of self-actualization before slipping into the Zorro outfit, grabbing the jar of peanut butter and making love like normal people.

· · ·

Dear Uncle Mike,

I'm writing to you not about myself, but about my younger brother. 'John' is thirty-six and recently divorced after a nine year marriage to a platinum plated (female dog). He suffered much and the family suffered with him. Thank God there were no children. We all suspect she would have eaten them anyway. 'Veronica', or as we called her, 'the ice queen', needed always to be center stage. No one's needs or interests came before hers and a more manipulative and controlling woman you'll never meet. I could tell you stories that would curl your hair but for purposes of brevity I won't. She is, thank heaven, no longer our problem. 'John' is. The divorce was final a year ago and he is still single. To my knowledge, he has not even seriously dated. My sister and I have introduced him to several women with no results. Our brother is a decent and attractive man who makes a good living and has a nice home and I know for a fact that women are interested in him. When I ask him when he's going to find himself a wife and settle down, he says he's waiting for the right woman to come along. I can understand why he would need some time to get over a horrible marriage but I'm afraid that avoiding pain by being alone could become a habit with him. He says he's happy being a bachelor but the family doesn't buy it. The ice queen used to tease him about being a closet homosexual. We always thought she was just being vicious but now we wonder if 'John' has a life we don't know about. Our mother is in complete denial and refuses to discuss the possibility and the situation is creating a great deal of pressure in the family. Should my sister and I simply confront him? Any insight you might have would be very much appreciated.

Concerned Sister, e-mail

Dear Sister,

Uncle Mike is, since you asked, happy to put in his two cents worth but doubts very much you'll appreciate it. You should leave your brother the hell alone. Unless you have proof he's unhappy living without a woman, let alone those selected by you and your equally presumptuous sister, you have no reason to assume his life is broken and in need of your fixing. Let the poor man be. If what you say is true, for nine long years his life was run by a woman who knew better than he what was good for him. What makes you think he needs another one to fill the emptiness created by the chance to make his own decisions? Living alone is not a symptom of anything more than a natural need for solitude; a concept which, owing to your unresolved control issues and a neurotic reluctance to mind your own business, might be difficult for you to grasp. You wonder if 'John' has a life you don't know about. Uncle Mike hopes so with all his heart but doubts it would be possible. In closing, he finds it interesting you make no mention of the opinions of your father, who could of course be dead, or your husband, who could easily come to welcome it.

• • •

Dear Uncle Mike,

I need your advice. I'm a twenty-three year old woman and I get hit on a lot by guys. This wouldn't be a problem but I just got out of a year long relationship and I'm not interested in dating right now. Guys I know get their feelings hurt when I tell them I'm not interested. How do I let them know it's nothing personal? I try but whatever I say doesn't work.

Please Don't Print My Name, Elko, Nevada

Dear Please,

Whatever Uncle Mike suggests probably won't work either. Not to worry. If men got a buck every time they were turned down by a pretty woman, none of them would need to work. The idea is to let the lads save face. One of Uncle Mike's favorite rejections was delivered by Audrey Hepburn to Cary Grant: "I'm sorry, I already know so many people that until one of them dies I couldn't possibly meet anyone else." If necessary, it's okay to stretch the truth. "I'm not interested in a relationship just now, but when I am I'll hunt you down like an animal." When all else fails, simply smile sadly and say, "Thank you, but I've got to draw the line somewhere."

• • •

Dear Uncle Mike,

For the last month, I've been having lunch, perhaps once a week, with a man from my office who is married. If it matters, he's forty-seven and I'm twenty-eight. We've worked in the same office for more than a year but have only recently been working on the same project. He knows that I know he is married, there is no subterfuge or 'cheating' going on. As marriages go, his is a happy one and I have no intention of doing anything to threaten it. The problem is that we've begun not quite flirting with each other. It's all innocent and it's more like brother sister teasing than anything else. Nothing more than a hug has ever passed between us. The real problem is the people we work with, most notably a woman who knows both of us. She says no matter what, it doesn't look right and sooner or later it's going to cause trouble somewhere. I don't care what others think, I enjoy this man's company and plan to continue to have lunch with him. I have complete faith in our ability to keep things on a friendship level. Am I, in your opinion, being naïve?

C.S., e-mail

Dear C.S.,

No, in Uncle Mike's opinion you're being stupid. There are no innocent flirtations; there are only flirtations that aren't consummated. Since you say there is no subterfuge or, heaven forbid, 'cheating' going on, Uncle Mike assumes your friend's wife knows about your lunches and that the two of them have chuckled good naturedly about your brother-sister relationship. She must be one heck of a woman. How else could we account for the fact that her marriage to the man who's flirting with you is, as marriages go, a happy one. Suddenly Uncle Mike is very tired. While it's good not to be overly concerned with how things look to others, it's also good to remember that, if everyone says you're behaving like a weasel, there's a very good chance you are. So many of life's confusions and troubles disappear when people encourage each other to behave well; to be, in sadly antiquated terms, ladies and gentlemen. A lady, which is to say a woman with more than a thimble full of class, would deftly discourage the 'attentions' of a married man and would throw herself onto a bonfire of vanities before playing the coquette for him. But we were talking about you. During your next innocent lunch, ask your friend if he has a photo of his wife. That way you'll have a face to picture while you sharpen your claws on someone else's marriage.

• • •

Dear Uncle Mike,

What is it that makes human beings so arrogant, Uncle Mike? How is it that we feel we have the right to summarily dismiss another creature's life?

Several weeks ago, a little cat showed up on my front porch. Being me, I went out and tried to make friends with it. I succeeded. Inquiries at our community Lost & Found turned up no distraught owners. Attempts to secure a new home elsewhere for this little cat failed. So, my husband and I decided to keep the cat ourselves.

Last Saturday, I took the cat the vet and received terrible news.

The cat has leukemia. This did not look like a sick cat. He ate, slept, played and purred like a healthy cat. But he had this disease inside him that would eventually kill him. And worse, he could spread the disease to other cats.

This was a sweet, quiet cat. He was loving, affectionate, he was beautifully colored. He was only 7 or 8 months old. Today, my husband took him to the vet to be put to sleep. My husband and I agonized over this decision. Our hearts have never been so sick and sore. I can't even kill spiders, Uncle Mike; I loathe them, but I take the time to capture them in a jar and dump them outside rather than squish them. Sitting down and discussing the imminent death of this sweet creature was the most horrible thing I've ever done. And it makes me angry. Most of the people we've talked to about this said the same thing: what we're doing is merciful.

I know that, in effect, this cat was already dying. I know that, once he became sick, he would have declined slowly in a lingering death. None of that convinces me that we should label what we did as merciful. Who are we to dispense something that profound?

This little animal came to us and found kindness. Then we killed him. I feel like scum. And I miss my cat. His name was Gobi Desert.

Stricken, Winlock, Washington

Dear Stricken,

Interesting name for a cat. The only words of comfort Uncle Mike can give is that death is an appearance, not a reality. In a universe that is, at every point in spacetime, alive, there is no room for anything more drastic or final than change. The organizing principle that was your cat is, as we speak, once again organizing bits of living matter into a vehicle designed to experience itself. That's what it was doing when it showed up on your doorstep and that's what it's doing now. The Cheshire cat is always smiling. As for spiders, Uncle Mike feels your pain. To counter his lack of compassion, he began calling them 'spiggles'. For better or worse, he now says good morning to them.

• • •

Hey Uncle Mike!

I'm a fifteen year old guy who has never been out on a date, kissed a girl (outside of relatives, and don't get any weird ideas). Yet for the past two or three years, I really want to have a relationship. I've tried to woo girls, but all my attempts have failed on account of shyness. Any ideas on how I can overcome my shyness, get a girl and a long relationship?

Web Nome (yes that is spelled to my liking), e-mail

Hey Web(!),

Uncle Mike is impressed with your ability to pose three tricky questions in a single sentence. His first suggestion is that you stop with the cute misspelling of 'gnome'. Gnomes, as you should know if you don't, are elementals; one of four different sorts of faeries (one for each of the elements) whose actions are the warp and woof of what we laughingly call reality: salamanders are faeries of the fire (spirit), sylphs are faeries of the air (mind), undines are faeries of water (emotion), and gnomes are faeries of earth (matter). As Uncle Mike understands the situation, your spirit, mind, and emotions are wooing their little hearts out but nothing happens in the material world. Go figure. As an experiment, why not play with the spelling of the other elementals and see which portion of your life turns to rubble?

Shyness has two sources: an underestimation of one's worth and an exalted estimate of how much time other people spend thinking about your shortcomings. You sound like an intelligent and sensitive fellow, if a little foolhardy when it comes teasing elves, and as long as you've not held back something important (an eye in the middle of your forehead for instance, or a tendency to bark when you're excited), you have no reason to enter any situation backing up. You are who you are, there's no one in the universe like you and, regardless what you think, you're not chopped liver. As Kurt Vonnegut pointed out, we become who we pretend we are. Pretend you're not shy. Pretend you're on top of your game. Pretend you never made fun of gnomes. No, Uncle Mike is not encouraging you to be a phony. The world tends to give back the energy we give: smile and it smiles, snarl and it bites, mumble and it ignores you. If you don't want to be shy, practice self confidence. In front of a mirror if necessary.

Uncle Mike refuses to discuss 'getting' a girl and encourages you to do the same. You're looking for female companionship, not a car. Uncle Mike suggests you stop looking for anything at all and concentrate on the friendships and acquaintances you already have among the complementary sex. Be a good friend and a pleasant companion and, as sure as there are gnomes who hold grudges, the girl will find you. A helpful hint: things tend to happen to the extent we believe they will. There's a reason that faith is recommended so highly.

Your last question is a real doozy. If Uncle Mike knew the universal equation for a long relationship between boy humans and girl humans, he'd have retired to a cabin in the forest on his Nobel winnings. As you can see, he hasn't. Whatever answer there is lies in the concept of 'relationship': a system of at least two variables in which the state of one partially determines the state of the other. Friendships endure because both people involved are sensitive to each other's needs; which is to say, they care about one another at least as much as they care about themselves and put their care into words and action. Relationships last because both variables dance together around a constant of mutual respect and unshakable loyalty. Love endures because it makes unity out of diversity. Individual attempts to master this high magic account for most of the plots in the human comedy. It only becomes tragedy when you stop laughing.

Getting back to your real problem: the gnomes. Uncle Mike suggests you find a quiet spot under a tree, thank the forces of creation for giving you the breath to complain and, with a pure and humble heart, call your future to you.

· · ·

Dear Uncle Mike,

　　If you get an invitation in the mail that asks you to RSVP, is it socially acceptable to e-mail your response?

Deanna, Portland, Oregon

Dear Deanna,

　　Not to Uncle Mike. But then, he wasn't the one who picked out the invitations and thought warmly of you while hand addressing the envelope.

. . .

Dear Uncle Mike,

　　If you stood at the edge of the universe and looked out, what would you see?

Rick, Phoenix, Arizona

Dear Rick,

　　If the universe had an edge, which, being a four-dimensional sphere whose surface and center are everywhere, it doesn't, you'd probably see the back of your head.

. . .

Dear Uncle Mike,

　　I have several very close friends whom I dearly love, and I try to be helpful when they need someone to talk to. I seem to have a knack for really seeing the problems of a situation and providing practical and sensitive advice on how to solve them. My question for you is, does it ever just suck the life right out of you to help all of the people who come to you? How do you keep yourself from internalizing their problems? Does it ever just really frighten you that these people look to you for, and expect, WISE advice when you may sometimes feel like you are just flailing along in life yourself? I really try to be responsible with the trust that people place in me, but sometimes I feel like I just don't have much energy left over for myself. How do you insulate yourself from the needs of others and still be helpful?

Just Jess

Dear Jess,

The answer to your last question is, of course, that you don't. Insulating yourself from those who come to you for help is like making love with your clothes on: possible, but not the experience either of you was looking for. As for having the life sucked out of him, it's been some time since Uncle Mike was reduced to a husk by anyone's perspective of the human comedy; partly because few things are more interesting than what people do with their lives and partly because he's learned not to deal with emotional issues emotionally. In that direction lies madness, not resolution. But you know this: it's your rational empathy that draws the emotionally uncentered to you like iron filings to a magnet. They honor you with their trust, you honor them with your best shot, everyone does what they can.

Yes, knowing himself as well as he does, Uncle Mike often finds it amusing that anyone able to form a complete sentence would ask his advice about anything more critical than a new tie. He may not be flailing at life but he does have a nagging suspicion that, as far as wisdom goes, he could be unfolding a whole lot faster than he is. Given this, does the responsibility of giving his opinion frighten him? No. Generally speaking, people do what they want to anyway. Uncle Mike's responsibility (aside from being the very soul of compassion) is to, when asked, let them know if they're behaving like someone without the brains of a parsnip, point out their errors in reasoning, dissect their mistaken notions of reality, and suggest things they might do that would not only make more sense but feel better too. If Uncle Mike is having a good day, he tries to be nice about it.

Feeling as if there's nothing left for you doesn't mean you're giving too much; it means you're not getting enough in return. Either you've forgotten who or what it is that charges your batteries, you've given the world the impression you can run on empty, or you're too busy feeling put upon to notice your cup is half full. The solution is not to close yourself off but to open yourself more, to take everything that's offered and give everything you have. You might also try to stop whining.

• • •

About the Author

Michael Burgess is an author and columnist of indeterminate age who observes the human comedy from the safety of a small town on the Oregon Coast. A prize winning journalist, he was, for ten years, featured columnist for ***This Week Magazine*** in Portland and served as founding president of *Northwest Writers, Inc.*, the region's first organization for those who, ignoring the pleas of family and friends, insist on arranging words for a living. He currently writes two syndicated columns: Ask Uncle Mike, a weekly advice column for the especially desperate, and Blame It On The Stars, a monthly horoscope for those who never read them. He is the author of four books: ***'Magic and Magicians', 'Uncle Mike's Guide to the Real Oregon Coast'. Letters to Uncle Mike', and 'MORE Letters to Uncle Mike'.*** He likes many dogs and some children, prefers briefs to boxers and, in his largely unbroken blocks of spare time, continues his search for a unified field equation suitable for printing on a T-shirt.

Also by the Author:

Uncle Mike's Guide to the Real Oregon Coast
ISBN: 0-9657638-1-1 ($14.95)

There are many pretty guides to the Oregon Coast. This isn't one of them. The author is a native Oregonian who assumes you want the truth. An overly zealous travel industry, and the shameless lies of tourists too proud to admit their mistakes, have created a myth of the Oregon Coast as a holiday destination for the normal to silly, if not dangerous, proportions.

The author refuses to be part of this. He has no axes to grind, no rain gear or sedatives to sell. He doesn't care if you visit the Oregon Coast or not. He only wants the pain and sadness to end. His heart goes out to the gullible who flock here each year expecting things they'll never find: warmth, sunlight, some token shred of civilization. He sees them as victims of a cruel joke. It's one thing to live in a fool's paradise, another to travel great distances getting to it.

Letters to Uncle Mike
ISBN: 0-9657638-5-4 ($14.00)

The North Oregon Coast's sobering challenge to Ann Landers, Dear Abby and Miss Manners answers questions about life, love, and quantum reality from people who often wish they hadn't asked.

Is cohabitation among women and men workable? Should children be made to wear leashes? Do friends let friends have breast implants? Is homosexuality a fad? Should one call before dropping by? Why are men such jerks? Do octopi make good pets? How do you know when your mate's cheating on you? Why are potatoes called spuds? What do women really want? What makes special relativity special? Does time go faster when you're having fun? Does death have meaning in a quantum universe?

Uncle Mike answers them all with the sensitivity and compassion he reserves for anyone who's ask a complete stranger for advice.

Magic and Magicians
(Out of Print)
Published by Capstone Press

An introduction to magic for young readers

Uncle Mike's books are available at your local bookstore,
or order from:

Saddle Mountain Press
PO Box 1096
Cannon Beach, Oregon 97110
Phone (503) 436-2947
Fax (503) 436-8635

Email: saddlemountain@upperleftedge.com